Struggling Women Walking Strong

Bronwyn Heard

amazon publishing

Copyright © 2024 Bronwyn Heard

All rights reserved.

ISBN: 9798879544800

No portion of this book may be reproduced, stored in a retrieval system, or transmitted by any means—electronic, mechanical, photocopy, recording, scanning, or other—except for brief quotations in critical reviews or articles, without the prior permission of the publisher.

Colour photos (including front cover):

Val Oldfield

Cover Photograph

The yellows, oranges and reds of the vine are glorious
Even though it won't be long until
The vine is laid bare
the branches pruned hard against the core.
And yet the vine drinks water.
Its roots draw nourishment from the soil.
Because the day will come when
New leaves and new fruit burst from new canes.
Growing strong.

Acknowledgements

To the women who have shown me how women grow strong

Lynnie Layland
Vivian
Lorraine Lovitt

And the strong women in my journey

Roslyn McGuire
Rosie Fisher
Lyn Cleasby
Margy Reyne
Sasha Langley
Anna Geary
Tanya Roberts
Dee Gadsby
Yvonne Griese
Anna Wallace
Kylie Iseli
Linda Hoskins
Karen Tebbet
Di Adamson

I am grateful and indebted to Blair Parke for her wise feedback and editorial skills and her encouragement to me as a new author.

Thanks to Val Oldfield for her beautiful photographs that bring so much joy.

Thanks to my husband Rod Heard for his wonderful support in all things and for his remarkable publishing skills.

Introduction

These are the stories of women who walked through life struggles and became strong. Some of them are not remembered as great women of history—but they are remembered. The reason to write these stories has been to look at the lives of these women and the issues they experienced. While these are the stories of ancient women, the issues are also today's issues. This book is a reflection of the way a group of women endured life struggles and became strong—not everyone does.

Part One are stories as these women may have remembered them and told their own stories, or the story of a friend, to others.

Part Two are studies of women in their time. Within their own circumstances and culture, I have explored their spirituality (or none) and their contribution to history, told through the biblical accounts and commentaries written about them.

The lives of these women are explored in their experience of disasters and triumphs, their struggles and recoveries, living through timeless issues. Some are stories of faith, while others are stories of people of resilience.

They were women who struggled with tough circumstances, but who became strong through their own journeys.

There are some links between the women, which we don't often hear about:

- Tamar and Rahab were foreign brides.
- Naomi brought another foreign bride, Ruth, back home to eventually marry Rahab's son, so Rahab and Naomi were both Ruth's mothers-in-law. They may have known each other as they lived with their families in the same small town, though Rahab had Boaz late in life, and Boaz would have been middle-aged at least when he married Ruth.
- Through Ruth, Rahab and Naomi became the great-great grandmothers of David, who is the most famous king of the Jewish nation, Israel.
- Ruth's grandchildren lived in the land of Canaan during the years that Deborah was the first female national leader (judge and prophet) of Israel.
- Bathsheba and Abigail were part of the same family because they

had the same husband (the same David, King of Israel), though they lived in different households.
- Eve, Tamar, Rahab, Naomi, and Bathsheba are all part of the ancestry of Jesus.
- Elizabeth was the cousin of Mary and Jesus's aunt.

There are other women who were critical to these women's stories.

- For Tamar, Leah also experienced their family violence.
- For Deborah, Jael is her second follower.
- Elizabeth shares her time of pregnancy after infertility with Mary during and after her unmarried teenage pregnancy.

The opportunity to write about these different women is to imagine and open their journeys up for view. We don't see enough of them. I have had the chance to study really interesting characters–to read each character in their historical context and describe it. In the stories, there is a little faction to flesh out minimal available information. The stories, though, are as close to the records as possible and are shared as authentic as is possible.

Through all of their stories, they have strengthened my faith and shown me that it isn't the journey or the triumphs or tragedies. It is the thread of a life woven through time that demonstrates how God provides in times of abasement and in times of abundance.

He keeps His commitments to us because He loves us.

This encourages me.

I trust that all of these women's stories touch and encourage you.

Themes covered in this book

Part 1 6
Grief and Loss (Bathsheba) 13
Businesswoman (Abigail)..25
Prostitution (Rahab) 39
Divorcee (Samaritan woman) 49
Losing the Perfect Life (Eve) 55
Infertility (Elizabeth)..63

Part 2 75
Mixed Cultures (Hagar)...79
Family Violence (Tamar) 89
Bitterness (Naomi) 101
Risky Politics (Esther)...107
Leadership (Deborah) 119

At the end of the book:
History Dates..128
Reference Books...129
Bible References 131

Part One

Introduction to Part One

The stories in Part One are written as if they are told by a narrator. That is, the story is written as if one person is sitting with you and telling their own story, or they are telling someone else's story to you.

Bathsheba was a woman who lived in Israel in about 1000 BC, in the time when David was the king. David was the second King of Israel after Saul, and after many decades when the country had been led by a prophet or judge. I am the narrator of Bathsheba's story and want you to know that the common portrayal of Bathsheba as an adulteress is unfair and untrue. Bathsheba lived through circumstances and losses that were overwhelming and became an influential woman of her time because of it. I hope you will see the people and strategies that helped her to grow from struggling to strong.

Abigail was a woman who lived in Israel around 1020 BC. Abigail was David's second wife. She married him before he became the King of Israel and during the time he was hiding from King Saul, who was trying to assassinate David. David is the narrator of her story, telling the reader about when he first met Abigail. Abigail was the wife of an abusive man at the time, and she showed strengths within a very tough marriage, even running the family business. The second half of the story is written as if Abigail is telling her own story about being married to David when she (and others) was kidnapped. This event in Abigail's life is not very well-known, so I hope you will see how Abigail used her strengths as she lived through tough times to become strong.

Rahab was a prostitute who lived in Jericho about 470 BC. At the same time, the Israelite nation (about four million of them) crossed the Jordan River from the desert country and invaded the country we now know as both Israel and Palestine. It was the beginning of conflict in that region, which continues today. Rahab's story is narrated by herself and covers the siege and war between the people of Jericho and Joshua's army of Israelites. She is telling her story of survival and courage. I hope you see her strengths and see how she is valued and honored through this experience.

We don't know the name of the divorcee from Samaria. She lived at the same time as Jesus and met Him in AD late 20s. Samaritans were a despised minority race in Israel at that time. The woman from Samaria is telling her own story of a woman who has lived in a racially vulnerable community and has been married (and divorced) four times. She, like many so many others, gets on with life as best she can. Her story shows us that Jesus "has our back," and we are each a missionary in whatever our circumstances are. We have the respect of God to be His hands and feet where we live.

Eve was created by God at the beginning, as the first woman. The story of Eve has inspired my use of photographs of the natural world in this book. It is amazing! Eve is telling her own story of Eden and of life after Eden: a perfect life and an imperfect life. Of struggling with an imperfect family and of becoming the mother, grandmother, and great- (great) grandmother to many. I think that Eve modelled a godly life as much as it was possible for her to do in her thoughts, actions and showing God's love and care towards each person in her family in her imperfect world.

I hope you will feel a desire to be a model of the kind of person you want your children to become as they live their own lives and make their own choices.

Elizabeth was an old woman at the time that Jesus was born in about 4 BC. She was a cousin of Jesus's mother, Mary. Elizabeth's story is narrated by Mary as she might have told the story to Luke, who wrote the book of Luke in the New Testament. I hope you will see Elizabeth as a woman who lived a life of infertility with energy, living a full and satisfying life; a woman growing in strength. I hope you will see her as a woman very well-prepared to be a mentor and support to Mary and be thrilled for her that she was gifted with John and was able to shower him with her mothering skills and love.

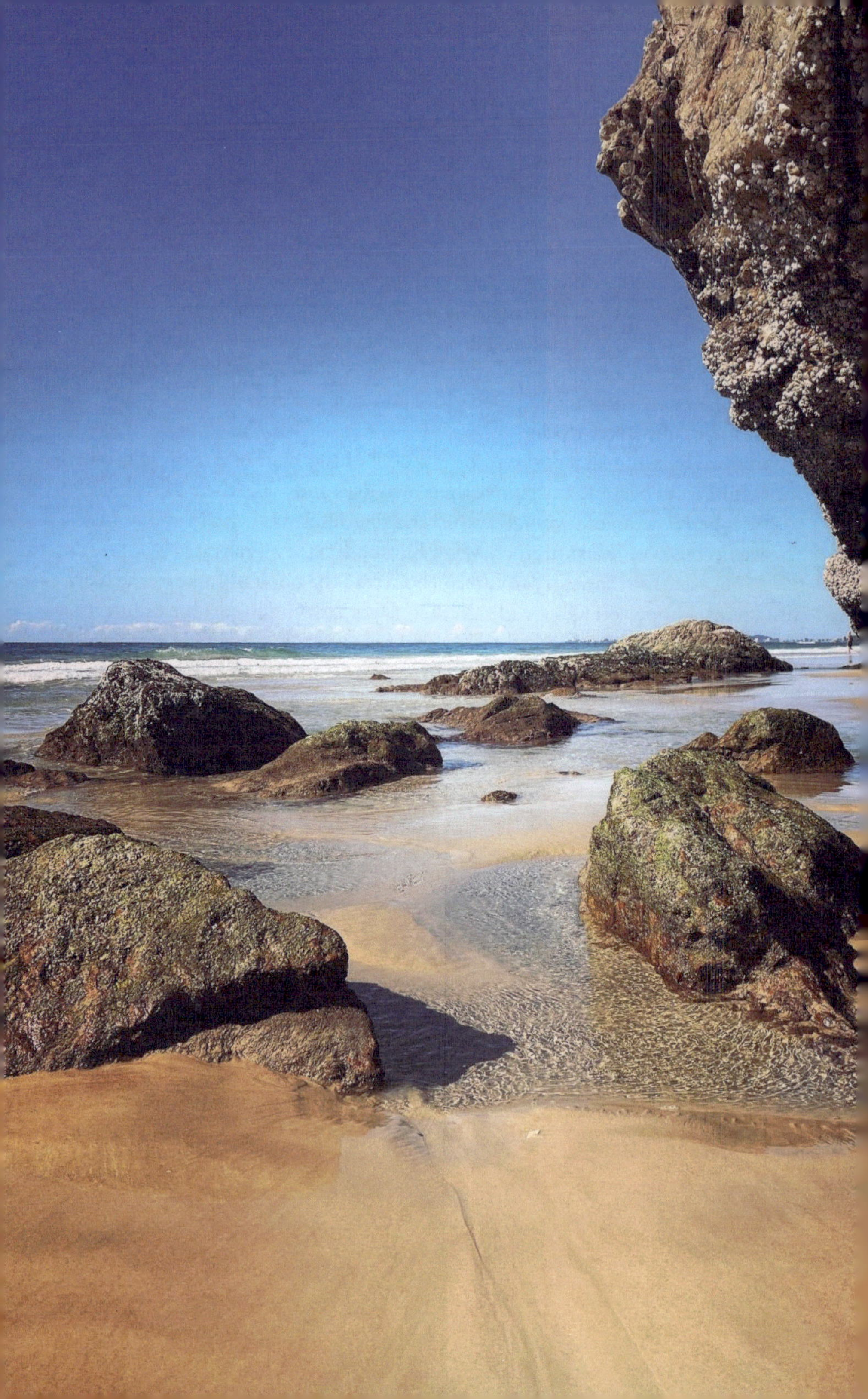

Bathsheba

Early 1000s BC

In the end, she slept with him.
It was easier than an ugly scene. Who would believe that she hadn't grabbed the chance anyway?
Hundreds, no thousands, of other women dream about him and would say "Yes" to sex in an instant—sexiest man alive!
With his national power, war hero, celebrity status—she worried she would find herself in a situation far worse if she said "no"...
Could it hurt the situation of her family?
They had worked hard to build their position in the city.
She thought the invitation was to a function or a lavish party...
He was famous, wealthy, married.
Getting the invitation had been so exciting.
Her friends wanted all the details—
Who had been there?
What did everyone wear?
Did she get to meet him?
Did he talk to her?
Instead, it turned out to be an intimate setup for two.
How did she get it so wrong? How was she going to get through the evening being friendly, keep the conversation light, save face, and leave without offence?
It hadn't worked.
He had been charming, insistent. The time wore on until the inevitable couldn't be delayed any longer. She'd been used.
Within weeks, the nightmare started.
The waking up sick,
tingling breasts
... a period missed.
Her husband, a man's man in the army, was away in action. So, she sent a message to David: "I'm pregnant to you. My husband has been away for months."
David was the army chief. He arranged leave for her husband.
A night or so at home would sort their problem out.

Her husband Uriah, though, declined to go home at all because the action was "too hot," and he couldn't leave his unit and take some leave with his wife. He'd made a short visit to the city to give a report to the chief but went straight back to this posting.

Bathsheba didn't see him.

She knew she was trapped; it would be over when he got home. His parents, her parents—they would all know. They'd want to know who the father was, and she would bring shame, disrespect, and divorce with the news.

Who's the father? He's the country, the nation–the king.

Would they believe her? If they did, how would they react? She knew. What was she doing getting herself noticed? She didn't even know how that happened—even to this day!

Every day was more of the nightmare and no answers.

****

The army official at the door said, "I'm sorry to have to inform you that your husband has been killed in action." He'd given her the official letter.

Uriah. Her husband.

She had first seen him from afar and thought he was handsome. As she'd watched over weeks and months, she'd liked him—he was honest, a leader who had an easy and loud laugh. He'd make a great husband.

When they had formally met, he had been blown away—she was stunning. He had wanted her, and he had married her.

No doubts for him.

They had a life together in the high-end social set of young adults and a future with good prospects.

All gone.

She was pregnant, a widow with someone else's baby.

Her sorrow and bereavement were deep. She had lost a man who adored her. Uriah had come to fight for a successful king. She had lost him.

Lost loving arms ... a man with passion, loyalty, the man's man. Her security.

The official mourners, the days of preparation, the funeral, the people–family, colleagues, well-wishers–all a blur.

She felt herself walking through days like treacle.

After the funeral, so many questions

and changes.
"Stay with us, dear."

The last of Uriah's income ... the need to work, earn an income.
Needing a place to live with the baby.
The baby. Loss.
The shame.
It was her closest friend who loyally filled her in about the gossip.
The dates were wrong. Uriah was away when the pregnancy started.
Friends, family, neighbors.
All gone.

Uriah. So sorry. He didn't deserve that.
Their life together taken away forever.

****

It had been easy to accept moving to the king's house.
When the formalities were done, she was another wife. She had security for herself, and more importantly, her baby.
That was the bottom line–providing for her baby.

****

Seeing that tiny face for the first time was amazing.
Those big eyes and tiny lips.
Hair plastered to smooth skin—after the first bath, that shock of hair stood straight up–a downy halo that looked soooooo cute!
Touching those tiny fingers and toes—the grip of that little hand around your finger.
For Bathsheba, the miracle of her new baby was soon replaced with a helpless agony of watching her baby's struggle to live.
Her baby's tiny nostrils flared, his tiny chest heaved, his little weak breathing grunts filled her with exploding agony.
What could she do except to cuddle and comfort?
Drop after drop of milk into that tiny mouth too weak to suck for more than a minute.
It broke her heart,
her whole life.
The household priest came to see her. Her baby was dying.
In her pain, she told her story—everything. I think the priest put his arm

around her shoulders and did not judge, but comforted her and prayed with her.

Then he told David the story he'd been told.

The truth.

This is what he said.

"There were two men in a city. One was very rich, owning many fields of sheep and herds of goats. The other was poor by comparison, owning nothing but a lamb he had managed to buy. He loved it and fed it from his own plate and let it drink from his own cup. He cuddled it in his arms like a baby.

Recently, a guest arrived at the rich man's house. But instead of killing a lamb from his own flocks for the traveler, he took the poor man's lamb and roasted it and served it."

The priest, Nathan, believed Bathsheba.

David could see what he was saying, and he knew it was true. Nathan explained the parallel to what David had done.

Nathan said to David:

"Why did you do this evil thing? You had Uriah killed in battle. You let the Ammonites kill him, and you took his wife."

2 Samuel 12:9 (Good News Bible)

David went to the place where the baby and Bathsheba stayed.
And then he saw her.
He saw a beautiful girl who had lost everything because of him.
He saw
    Her broken heart breaking
    Holding their dying baby.
It broke him up. He joined her in grieving. You can read it in 2 Samuel 12:16.

****

What's it like for a mother when her baby dies?
Skin so soft.
So peaceful. Too still.
His little body looked so perfect. How can this death be real?
Feeling the coolness of death replacing the warmth of life.
Willing your own arms' warmth to deny it.
An agony of what might have been, could have been, should have been.
Time lost.
Letting that tiny treasure go from your arms.

The moment when no breath can enter your chest
and oxygen leaves every cell, every muscle.
Your legs can no longer hold your body up.
arms uselessly there
Lying numb and empty.
Why does your life go on?

Part of yourself will always be buried in that tiny box.
Buried deeply.

The emptiness of the days.
Empty hands–prepared and wasted.
The pain a baby's cry brings.
The ache of others' joy.
Birthdays pass.
Then years of tears.
Loss.

When the baby died, David took on his responsibilities for Bathsheba. He cleaned himself up from his mourning. He got his things in order. He went to Bathsheba and comforted her. He was part of her recovery.

He publicly apologized for the shame he caused by taking her when she was someone else's wife. This is the poem to God he published.

O loving and kind God
Have mercy
Have pity on me and take away the
Awful stain of what I did wrong.
Wash me
Clean me up of this guilt.
Let me be pure again.
For I admit my shameful action
—it haunts me day and night.
It is against you that I have done the wrong thing
I have done this terrible thing.
I see it all and your sentence is just, even though
I was born imperfect, from the moment
my mother conceived me.
You deserve honesty from the heart

Yes, with sincerity and truthfulness
Oh, give me this wisdom.
Sprinkle me with cleansing blood
And I shall be clean again.
Wash me and I shall be whiter than snow.

And after you have punished me,
Give me back my joy again.
Don't keep looking at what I did wrong
Wipe them from your sight.

Create in me a clean heart, Oh God,
Filled with clean thoughts and right desires.
Don't toss me away
Don't take your Holy Spirit from me.
Restore to me the joy of your salvation
And make me willing to obey you.

Then I want to teach your ways to others
And those, who have the same problems as me
Will be able to be sorry and return to You.

Don't sentence me to death
Oh, my God, you can rescue me
Then I'll sing that you have forgiven me
My lips will be unsealed and I will praise you.
You don't want penance
If you did, I'd gladly do it.
You aren't interested in gifts
Burned on altars.
It is a broken spirit you want
Remorse and sorrow
A broken and sorry heart
Oh God, you won't ignore.

And Lord, don't punish my country
For what I did wrong
Help your people and protect our city.

And when my heart is right

You will rejoice in the good I do
And the way I worship you.

Loss and grief changed over years. A few years later, when Bathsheba nursed another baby boy that she and David named Solomon, and on the anniversary of her baby's death, she would take a moment to remember.

Four

How much I miss you, baby boy.

Our family is a little different to what it would have been. We will never have that family painting done of all our children together, but having my little sketch of you when you were just a few hours old is the most precious thing.

I carry around your fingerprint charm everywhere we go so you are always with us.

I haven't had much time to stop and grieve today, but I'll squeeze Solomon a little tighter, feel him breathing in and out while he sleeps on my chest, and I'll hug him a little longer during those sleepy nighttime feeds because I remember how desperately I wished for those things with you four years ago.

I will celebrate you today with a little cake and add another charm to your bracelet.

Until I can hold you in my arms again,

I love you, baby boy.

Adapted from a poem by Anna Geary

Walking Strong

Life continued for Bathsheba. I don't think she did it alone.

We know David mourned with her, comforted her, publicly took the shame she had been carrying.

We know the prophet Nathan maintained his relationship with their family over the years, and particularly relied on Bathsheba in the leadership decision about David's heir.

Bathsheba lost her husband and her baby in less than twelve months.

Did Bathsheba move on? That's what people say, isn't it, after the death of a spouse, a boyfriend, a child? "Moving on" carries a sense of putting the person behind you. Did her family and friends think she would put the life she had in the past, not think about them anymore? Would she let her grief go and not grieve anymore?

Some people talk about taking their pasts into the future and "moving forward." They talk about taking their past experiences that have made them who they are forward into a new life. They still have people who are important to their personal lives and histories, interests, intelligence skills and knowledge, and all of these make up the person moving forward.

Bathsheba was able to move forward.

She had experience as a wife; that was still part of who she was. She took her way of being a wife into her new marriage to David.

I think Bathsheba decided to build a good marriage with David (in the context of being one wife among many hundreds, as well as hundreds of concubines). I think she nurtured Nathan's support over the years and built her own influence through these men. We know that Bathsheba, in later years, held a position of respect with David, Solomon, Nathan, and the court. She was instrumental in securing the throne for Solomon.

In her struggle, Bathsheba showed a capacity to recover and become strong. How did she do this?

She didn't take heroic actions, but she acted in the face of the problems. She didn't hide the truth of her experience, but chose specific people to talk to, and she listened to good counsel.

She accepted help.

She moved forward.

She became a person with strong character.

We each have been created with in-built strength.

Some aren't able to see or use their strength, and some pretend that the things they face aren't impacting on their lives.

Strength, some of the time, comes from admitting when we are failing, telling someone, and not only asking for help but taking it when it is offered.

We know that David and Bathsheba had other children together. They named one of their sons Nathan after the prophet (1 Chron. 3:5). Solomon was their fourth son. When Solomon was born, David named him. Nathan also visited the family and gave Solomon a second name–Jedidiah, meaning "Beloved of the Lord." He was Solomon Jedidiah.

I think Bathsheba treasured the children who were born to her. I think being a great mother was the most important part of her life.

As an adult, Solomon was given the gift of wisdom, and some of his wise counsels were recorded as the book of Proverbs.

In Proverbs, he wrote a number of things about his mother:

1:8 "Listen to your mother and father. What you learn from them will stand you in good stead; it will gain you many honors."
3:1 "My son, never forget the things I've taught you. If you want a long and satisfying life, closely follow my instructions."
4:3 "For I, too, was once a son, tenderly loved by my mother as an only child, and the companion of my father."
15:20 "A sensible son gladdens his father. A rebellious son saddens his mother."
17:26 "A man who mistreats his father or mother is a public disgrace."
22:6 "Teach a child to choose the right path, and when he is older, he will remain on it."

Was one of Bathsheba's strengths that she learned wisdom and was known for providing wise counsel? Her nation had Job's book and knew that the beginning of wisdom is the fear of the Lord.

Bathsheba would have understood Job and the losses he faced, including living through the death of his children.

Solomon describes wisdom throughout this book and refers to wisdom as "she." I think he was giving examples of how his mother lived her life.

Here are some of the poetic ways Solomon describes the Lady of Wisdom:
"Wisdom, better than all the trappings of wealth,
nothing you could wish for holds a candle to her.

I am Lady Wisdom, and I live next to Sanity.
Knowledge and Discretion live just down the street.

> The fear of God means hating Evil,
> whose ways I hate with a passion–
> pride and arrogance and crooked talk.
>
> Good council and common sense are my characteristics,
> I am both Insight and the Virtue to live it out.
> With my help, leaders rule,
>
> And lawmakers legislate fairly.
>
> I love those who love me,
> Those who look for me find me.
> Wealth and Glory accompany me—
> also, substantial Honor and a Good Name.
>
> You can find me on Righteous Road–that where I walk-
> At the intersection of Justice Avenue,
>
> Handing out life to those who love me,
> Filling their arms with life–armfuls of life!*
>
> *Extracts from The Message Proverbs 8:12-21

Questions for Reflection

The death of a baby has a profound impact on a parent. What were the strategies and support that you know of that means a person has moved forward after a personal tragedy?

The death of this baby united Bathsheba, Nathan, and David. How can we become known for what unites us? What would we have to do?

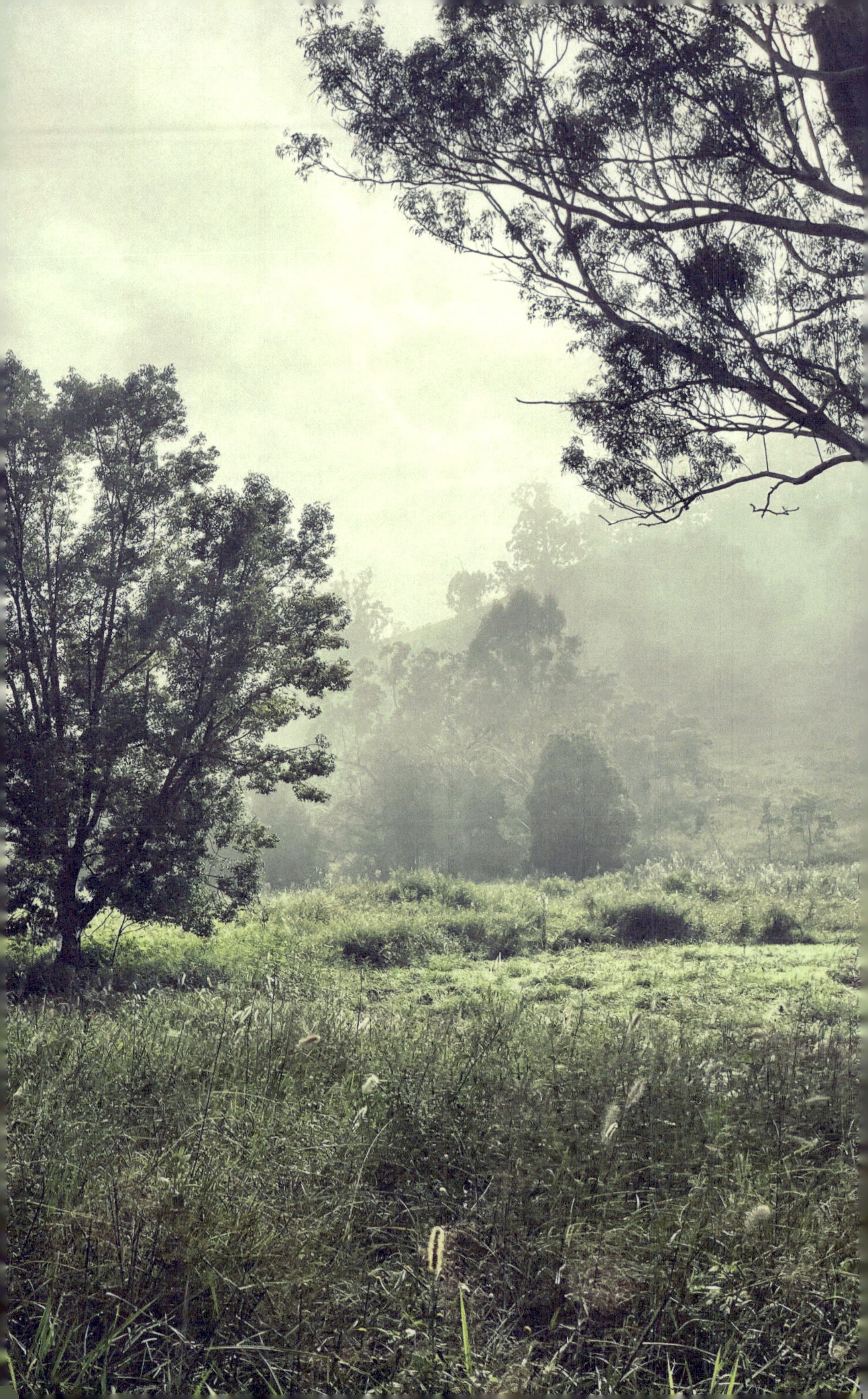

Abigail

Late 1020s BC

There are certain privileges in life that should never be taken for granted, and meeting with Abigail is one of them. I went to see her a few days ago at her business quarters. It was the day after her husband died.

The woman was sitting—more ethereal and elegant than the most fevered imagination might have allowed for, and we discussed privileges of her kind:

Like the dispensation of living an authentic life;

a life of meaning.

Like the favor of her personal assistant who said to me at the door, "This woman rules her place and I said to her this morning, 'I just want to say God bless you as you have blessed us, and He has blessed us through you.'"

Like the extraordinary mystery of her-, she is so other-worldly that it makes people she works with understand there is more in all of us than meets the eye.

Like her purpose and courage to support the people on her team to be the best that they can be; to thrive; to learn their "fields of fascination" and build their life work around it.

****

The first time I met her, I was preparing for a battle with an obtuse guy called Nabal. I was fired up with my anger and said to my men,

"It's been useless – all my watching over this man's property in this wild deserted area so that nothing of his was missing; and he has paid me back evil for good. May God do to me, and more so, if by morning I leave alive one male of all who belong to him."

1 Samuel 25:21,22 NIV

And just as I said it, our scout called a warning. We stood as one, ready to face the foe. We saw glimpses of colour as the rider sped through the trees down the hillside toward us. The sounds grew louder as the animal darted between the trunks. The rider came through the clearing onto the road, reining the beast to a noisy stop. The rider, a woman, leaped nimbly down without aid and threw back her hood, revealing a mane of thick, shining hair. Even under a gloomy sky, it appeared shot through with golden highlights. She was tall, her face finely chiseled, high cheekbones, and a strong, though not masculine, jaw.

It was the man's wife.

She saw me, took several steps forward, fell to her knees, and bowed low in front of me.

The words tumbled out of her mouth.

"My Lord, let the blame be on me alone. Please let me speak to you. May my Lord pay no attention to this ill-natured fellow, Nabal. He is just like his name and his head has been foolish in his dealing with you. He has acted like an idiot. But as for me, your servant, I did not see the men that you sent to request help with food provisions. Now since the Lord has kept you, my master, from bloodshed and avenging with your own hands, as surely as the Lord lives, and as you live, may your enemies and all who intend to harm you be like my husband Nabal.

"And let this gift, which I as your servant am bringing to her master, be given to the men who follow you. Please forgive my offence, for the Lord will certainly make a lasting dynasty of your house because you are fighting the Lord's battles.

"Let no wrongdoing be found in you as long as you live.
If anyone stands in your way,
If anyone tries to get you out of the way,
Know this. Your God-honored life is tightly bound
in the bundle of God-protected life;
But the lives of your enemies will be hurled aside
as a stone is thrown by a sling.

When God completes all the goodness he has promised you and sets you up as the prince over all of Israel, you, my master, will not have guilt as a dead weight on your heart – the guilt of an avenging murder.

"And when God has worked things for good for you, remember me."

1 Samuel 25:24-31 NIV

I was stunned—she knew all about me, even about slaying the Philistine giant with my sling! And she was prophesying, predicting that I would definitely become the next king. She was declaring a Davidic dynasty for our country! Had she heard that the Prophet Samuel had anointed me to be the next king? She must have known I was on the run!

To my amazement, as she spoke, her servants arrived on the road behind her with mules loaded high with hundreds of loaves of bread, two full skins of wine, five sheep dressed reading for cooking, a bushel of roasted grain, and hundreds of raisin and fig cakes. It was a feast!

And, for my part, that was the end of the matter.

Abigail, the gracious and strategic wife of Nabal, had saved him from being killed (which had been my plan) because she knew how to deal with both of us.

The hardness of the man and the kindness of the wife struck me. (A thought crossed my mind that many an Abigail is tied to a Nabal.)

I said a number of things to her, but most importantly, I said,

"Praise God that you came out here to meet me. I pray that you are blessed because you have very good judgment. Go home in peace. I have heard what you have had to say, and I will honor your request."

One of the young men with me came to me as soon as she left. He told me that when he had gone with my group of messengers to ask for help from Nabal, one of the man's shepherds came to him as they were leaving and suggested he let the man's wife, Abigail, know that Nabal had been surly and mean at their meeting. My man decided there was nothing to be lost and went to the main house, where the shepherd took him to tell Abigail the whole story.

I was intrigued. I needed to know all about her.

I told my man to find out what he could by visiting the homestead in the days following. He talked to the staff there. And he saw her from time to time and was a willing investigator. He said to me,

"My Lord, to this captivated outsider there appears such absence of vanity in her, such grace and exuberance, that to know her is to fall in love with her."

I soon knew that she was a successful businesswoman. When she married Nabal, her business became tied in with her husband's and (along with his large farming holdings), he became influential in the local community of Carmel. After their marriage, it became apparent to her that she could not have confidence in his business dealings; the staff could see she looked sick in the stomach in many of his ruthless business deals. She worked quietly, repairing the damage—in her own way, she was far more influential than her husband.

Her action to prevent my revenge was not so quietly done. My man reported when he went to the house the next day that the servants were scurrying about in silence, the tension palpable. Nabal's angry shouting at his wife earlier in the day had gone on for hours and then, quite unexpectedly, he had a collapse of some sort.

Apparently, when she got back the previous day, she found her husband hosting an impromptu party, and he spared no expense throughout the evening—he was having a great time and was under the weather by the time she arrived, so she told him the next morning that the payback from David's army was averted.

Who is this person who was willing—and could withstand—that level of venom? I am compelled to look deep into this life to find out where the strength of character is in there. What kind of woman can stand up as a human being through years and years of malicious actions, and still maintain her convictions?

My man went back to the household a couple of times after that to see what would play out. Nabal stayed unconscious—still as a stone, for ten days, and then he died. On the day after he died, Abigail was meeting with the staff, preparing for the funeral, keeping business going.

My man was moved by it all–the person, Abigail, moved him.

He said to me,

"He [Nabal] was lucky enough to have, as the last vision of his life, her lovely face. She was by his side at the end. When I heard about that woman staying with him … there is nothing more compassionate than that. As great as she is in her work and in dealing with us, her compassion is what I think of when I think of her."

I visited her soon after the funeral.

There's something that's completely transparent about her, a glowing quality that's quite striking and delicate. She has a look like she has swallowed a lighted lamp.

I've come to see her again today.

I've come to propose marriage. If she says "yes," I'll send a formal request through my personal staff as soon as possible.

Walking Strong

We know that David's personal servant went to Abigail and said, "David has sent us to you to take you to become his wife."

And she responded with the local custom of welcoming them to her home by bowing low and saying,

"Here is your maidservant ready to serve you and wash the feet of my master's servants."

She treated all staff with the utmost respect—as equals in their humanity.

All was ready.

She mounted her donkey and, attended by her five maids, went with the warrior's servants to meet David and become his wife.

Abigail came into David's life just after Samuel, his mentor, supporter, and protector, had died. And at that time, David also was battling the ups and downs (mostly downs at that time) of his relationship with the ruler of Israel, King Saul. David needed safe havens because Saul was attempting to have him killed. Saul had given Michal, his wife and Saul's daughter, to another man, so David was newly separated.

Judette Gallares, a Pilipino nun, finds in Abigail's speech to David an intuitive application of four principles of active non-violence...

1. Recognizing any truth or goodness in the adversary's position.
2. Admitting any ways in which one has betrayed that goodness of the adversary.
3. Pointing out how everyone (including the adversary) will be badly affected by the adversary's proposed course of action.
4. Proposing how the adversary can participate in developing an alternate solution to the conflict.

(Gallares, J.A., 1992, Images of Faith: Spirituality of Women in the Old Testament, published by Maryknoll, N.Y., Orbis Books.)

Abigail was a woman who walked strong.

Their meeting was at the right time when David needed her good judgment and the support of the Carmel community who were loyal to her. Carmel was in Hebron, Judah, and marrying Abigail gave him a new power base among the inhabitants of Judah.

What made her walk strong?

- She lived authentically.
- She did not side with, or stay silent, about surliness, ruthless ways or meanness.
- She had a meaning and purpose for life. That is, she had goals for herself that she worked at.
- She did the best she could in tough situations and had down-to-earth common sense.
- She spoke wisely, with inner strength and concern for peoples' needs.
- She was an active advocate of non-violence and peace, an approach to leadership that relies more on the power of reconciliation and peace than on the power of hate and vengeance.
- She treated people with respect, knowing there is more in all of us than meets the eye.
- She was generous.

- She was up to date with the current events.
- She had a strong faith.
- She was clever and was able to use rhetoric effectively when she spoke initially to David to convince David that God would protect him and take vengeance on any of his enemies, so that his hands could remain free of bloodshed out of vengeance.
- She was loyal to her staff and received their loyalty.
- She showed fairness and integrity in her dealings, sharply contrasting with the surly and mean nature of her husband; and so, she had people's trust from all walks of life.
- She was a good manager, making sound judgments and making things happen—quickly and strategically when that was required.
- She was secure in her environment, having places of personal safety and financial security. She valued work outside the home.
- She was gracious and kind to people.

These are the qualities that make women beautiful. Jewish historians record Abigail as one of the four most beautiful women who have lived–the others being Eve, Rahab, and Esther.

****

Abigail remembers another chapter of her life with David

"It was hard saying goodbye to David yesterday in Jerusalem. So hard and such a relief! I was longing for home and peace.

I've woken this morning at home, and I've been drinking in the bird sounds, the quiet of the morning, and the gentle light of dawn over the hilltops and the peaceful land sloping down to the creek at the foot of the hill where our home stands. I can hear the morning start downstairs in the household, and I stretch luxuriously across the cool linen that embraced me when I fell wearily last night after the long ride home.

"What a time it's been–nearly ten years since our wedding day!

"I have time to remember...

Ours is a marriage that brought strength to both of us. By his marriage to me, David gained valuable property and business interests that I continue to manage.

"I got security for our family businesses and property, as well as status as the wife of the country's celebrity also anointed to be the next king of our country.

"And in no time at all, our son Chileab Daniel was born. He's a gorgeous two-year-old. He'll be up soon, and we'll have all day together checking that all our stock is well. We have calves and lambs coming soon—what fun to enjoy together. I can't wait to see him with those baby lambs!

"It's been a rocky road, especially those first two years.

"Within months of our marriage, David took another wife.

Mmmm... wasn't expecting that so soon.

When we married, he was separated from Michal, so I felt I was his only wife. The new marriage was an alliance arrangement with the Jezreel community. David has a strategic alliance with the Carmelites through his marriage to me, and a strategic alliance with the Jezreelites through Ahinodom, wife number three. She has her own household, her own life.

"And my Lord, he needed these alliances.

Why, you ask?

There were a few reasons.

"Only a year before, David had killed Goliath, the Philistine giant.

Across Israel, the youth sing this song with a chorus, 'Saul has killed his thousands and David his ten thousands.'

Yes, King Saul was jealous and, being the first king of the country, he was protecting his position as king of Israel.

It's our way in this part of the world.

David's first wife was King Saul's daughter, Michal—David's prize for killing 200 Philistine soldiers at war against Israel, not long after he killed Goliath. Michal and David separated when Saul began his mission to assassinate my husband, and Michel moved on to someone else.

"The Middle East has always been a violent place.

"David was hiding out behind enemy lines.

Then David took both of us wives and set up in Philistine lands with his 600 men, and he joined the Philistine army. He joined forces with a local prince, Ashish. His army grew with his reputation and successes.

"We were wealthy and became wealthier, expanding our family business in Gath country. With David busy in the army, I've continued to manage the business in our town, Zilzag. The town became prosperous in our first year here. Word got around, and there were spies in town.

"David said to me,

'I heard that Saul's spies at Ziph had told him where my hideout was so Saul took off like an arrow released from the bow and camped out just off the road at Hakilah Hill a few days ago. Our scouts came back with his camp location within hours.

Well into the night, I went down to check out the camp. There we were, watching Saul and his army generals talking as they settled down for the night. The security was pathetic. I said to the two guys beside me, "Who'll go into the camp with me?" Abishai went with me, and we crept right up to Saul–stretched out on the ground, his spear stuck in the ground beside his head, and his troops all asleep on all sides.

Abishai said, "Here's your chance. Let me nail him to the ground with his spear–one hit will do it. I won't need more than a second."

I told Abishai I would not kill Saul or have his blood on my hands. And then I grabbed his spear and his water jug, and we took off into the night.

Not a soul saw!

Not a soul knew!

No one woke up!

Then we raced across to the next hill. And I shouted, "Hey Abner! How long do I have to shout for you to wake up and protect the king? Look, I've got his spear and his water jug that were right beside his head!"

Then Saul yelled out, "Is that you, David?"

And I yelled back, "Yes, it's me, my King. What crime have I committed that you are hunting me? If I've wronged you, then I'll take a wrap. But if it's others telling you to hunt me down, shame on you."

David told me that Saul apologized so he gave him back his spear and water jug, and Saul went home.

"A couple of months later, the Philistine armies were preparing to fight against Israel, and they decided David's section were a risk in this battle–it really wasn't a surprise that they thought David and his men might find themselves with divided loyalties.

Prince Ashish sent him and all his soldiers home to Zilzag. We didn't know they were on their way home.

"At that time, I was at work, and our nursemaid was looking after little Dan at home. He was growing up so fast, heading towards two years old. There I was at the market, just finishing off a sale for our new season's heifers, when chaos broke out. I'll never forget it.

"Amalekite soldiers were everywhere, pouring through the town, rounding everyone up. When that was done, they loaded up all the goods in the markets and rounded up all the livestock.

"It took all day. I was hoping the nursemaid would have heard and taken

Dan into hiding, but no. Right on feed time, she came around the corner of our stall and so they were put with me in the pen—we would all be sold off as slaves on the trader road down south at that horrible market.

I wept.

"Ahinodom, David's other wife, was in that pen as well as all the other wives and children of Zilzag. Those soldiers knew the men were away with the army.

They marched us through the town going south and behind us. The whole town went up in flames.

Our home was gone.

"The days marching south were harsh. Our people stayed together. No mercy with these soldiers—anyone who was frail or got sick was left behind to starve to death in the arid countryside around that road south. On the second day, one of their Egyptian servants got sick. He was kicked to the side of the road into a rough sort of field. I reckoned he'd last less than a day under that beating sun. And we were driven on.

"Imagine the horror, shock, and anger when my husband and his six hundred men arrived home to find they were a day too late. Their town was razed to the ground, their wives and children kidnapped, their belongings and farming stock stolen.

David knew our baby Dan, Ahinodom, and I, like all the other men's families, would be on their way to be sold into slavery.

"The men were distraught. They wept and cried out their anguish.

Then they turned on David, my beautiful husband, blaming him. They really got fire under their bellies over their total loss and decided to kill David.

He got the local priest's support and negotiated with 600 of his men to go with him to try to get their families back.

"At the end of the first day's march, there was trouble brewing again when they reached the Besor Creek, so only 400 men continued with David. He would not stop.

"Early, the next morning they found that Egyptian servant beside the road, and David stopped, fed him, and gave him water for his thirst. When he had revived, David said to him, 'Who do you belong to?'

"Well, did that guy spill the beans!

David said to him, 'Can you take us to them?'

He said, 'Can I ever!'

"I was exhausted—we were five days into the march. None of us were getting much in the way of water and bread, and I was worrying about my milk drying up. Dan was nearly on to everyday food, but I didn't want him to eat the dirty stuff we were being given. Dan was such a good, little man, travelling in a wrap strapped to my back. I worried.

"After lunch, the soldiers decided to stop and party. They spread themselves out–eating, drinking, dancing all afternoon with the meat, wine, bread, and delicacies they had scored at Zilzag market.

"I was a little away from the group, taking a little privacy to feed my baby. Out of the corner of my eye, a man caught my attention. Just a little wave bidding me stay low. It was David!

I stayed exactly where I was. My spirit lifted.

"You know, by then, the soldiers didn't know whether they were Arthur or Martha. As the twilight started, David's men moved through the groups, lowering them to the ground as they went. Only one young group of lads realized what was up at the end, and they mounted up on the camels that were there and took off for their lives.

"As for us, David and his men recovered everything and took us all home. Not a single person was lost from our town.

Even better, we had more than what was taken from the town. Every family was reunited, and every family got their own things back. Then all the rest was shared out equally between everyone–the people who went in to battle and the people who didn't go with the men. David said, 'God has protected us and handed over forces that came against us. The share of the man who stayed with supplies is to be the same as that of him who went down to battle. All will share alike ... David made this a statute and ordinance for Israel from that day forward."

1 Samuel 30:21-25 NIV

"Though we had the town to rebuild, we were rich. The men put their energy to work and within weeks, we were settling back into life. I decided I'd had enough struggles to make me stronger. I was looking for a quieter life by then.

Did we get that?

Not yet.

"We knew the fighting was on between the Israelites and Philistines. Saul was determined to expand his lands. The Philistine army was strong, even without David's section. The battle turned in the Philistine's favor, and they raced into the center of the Israelite troops and killed Jonathan, David's best friend, and Jonathan's brother. They were the King's sons. Saul took an arrow and saw his battle was lost. He fell on his sword and died.

"Three days after we had returned to Zilzag after David rescued us from the slave camp, a man in tatters arrived and told David that Saul and Jonathan had died in the battle. My lovely man David cried and mourned for the loss of the King and for Jonathan. He said, 'O my dear brother Jonathan, I'm crushed by your death. Your friendship was so dear to me and your love toward me was wonderful, far exceeding anything I have known and ever hope to know" They had been through a lot together since their teens.

"David has just turned thirty. He told me about the time that Samuel had visited and anointed him to be the next king after Saul. The generals and the priest arrived as David expected.

They crowned him King at Hebron.

I was there!

****

"We've all been up at Jerusalem for the coronation celebrations there.
What excitement and pageantry we've been honored with by our people.
My husband is the King of Israel.
He is loved.
He is a great king who will be remembered throughout history.
He has brought peace to our nation.

"In a few weeks, he'll get away from the furious pace of the Court–so much to do as he begins his work for the country. He and Dan will spend time with the lambs. David's sure he will be a good shepherd–following after his dad.

Oh, the pride of a father for his firstborn is a joy to my heart.
"He's teaching Dan a favorite poem that David wrote while he was a young shepherd teenager on his father's property. They'll sing it together in the hills.

'The Lord is my Shepherd.
I shall not want.
He makes me to lie down in green pastures.
He restores my soul.
He leads me in the paths of righteousness,
For His name's sake.
'Even though I walk through the valley of the shadow of death
I fear no evil
For You are with me
Your rod and your staff
They comfort me.

'You prepare a table before me
In the presence of my enemies.
You anointed my head with oil
My cup overflows.
'Surely goodness and mercy shall follow me
All the days of my life
And I shall dwell in the house of the Lord forever.'"

Psalm 23

"I'm so happy. I live in peace."
Abigail did live in peace after that.
David reigned for forty years, and the nation lived in peace.

Questions for Reflection

Abigail's story is leadership with integrity. In management, these people are very hard to find in any organization. In thinking about leaders you know or have worked with, who have you noticed works consistently with integrity? What are their skills and behaviors that demonstrate their integrity?

What leadership qualities do you think David learned from Abigail that he used at other times in his life?

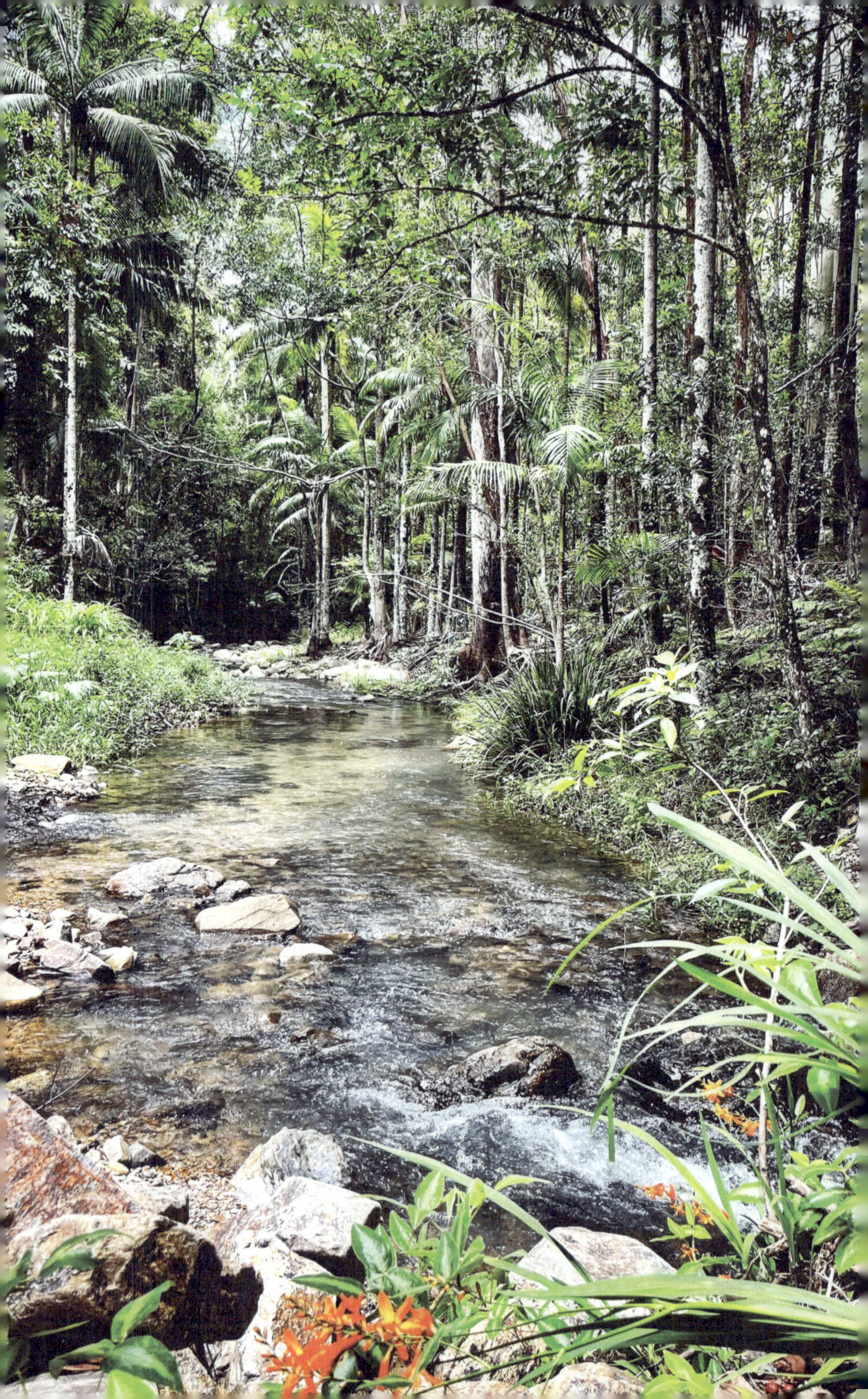

Rahab

Late 1470s BC

Ours is a family business; it started with my mother. She started as a novice and ten years later ran it. Eventually, she inherited it. My sister and I are working now full time in the business–the oldest trade in the world.

I don't remember any other life. The house has a regular rhythm–

Quiet mornings

—with the smell of fresh bread and eggs wafting from the kitchen. Mum, talking with the cook through her three cups of coffee. We get an extra helping from the cook before the staff drift in for their breakfasts. They all live on site, and everyone becomes family. From time to time, someone new joins the group. They are either down on their luck or running away. There's work for everyone.

After breakfast, there's the general cleaning of the rooms and the front parlor. Mum does the banking like clockwork every morning. Most people pay in cash. We don't keep cash on the premises, though—ˆit's asking for trouble.

Business usually gets going slowly.

Business–all day, every day

Sometimes we see customers in the mornings. Usually blow-ins, if you'll pardon the pun. We have our regular customers who keep to regular times, wanting their regular preferences. That's the best business.

We occasionally get an "out of town" guy that give girls a bad time. We don't want that sort of business. One sign of trouble, our men move those customers on.

The evenings pick up. Late in the evening is party time–drinks, hot finger food circulating, and music–always. We can work into the early morning, sometimes all night.

We get our quiet nights. I love them.

Weekends are really busy with the tourist trade.

Mum keeps it all together. On her nights off, it's up to me.

We don't get days off in this business.

The last few weeks, we have had two regulars who've booked for a few days at a time, but I know who they are. They are spies from the Israelites. Bedouins who've lived in the deserts since they escaped from Egypt forty years ago. We've heard all about them from the travelling trade caravans. They have turned their attention to Canaan, and towns all across the area are getting ready for war. More than that, I know these two men are spying out the lay of the city in the days they spend here.

One of the men asks for me, and his name is Salmon. We talk for hours about anything and everything. He is gentle and kind, and when I'm with him, I want time to last forever. I know I've let my guard down, and some days, I want to leave with him the next time they go–other times, I know I'm crazy to have these spies staying at the house.

Last night, they raced in the back door and went to their rooms and locked the doors. I told them they were out of their minds thinking they could hide there, and I took them up to the roof where they could hide between the flax that was laid out to dry on the roof. My whole household was in danger, and there was no way I was going to risk our lives this night.

Just to add to the stress of it all, it was Mum's night off, so it was up to me to block the soldiers when they came looking. One of them said,

"Bring the men out who are staying at this house. They're spies; they've come to spy out the whole country."

I said:

"Yes, two men have been here but I didn't know where they were from. Just a little while ago as it was getting dark and when the gate was about to be shut, I saw them slip out. I have no idea where they are going, but hurry – you could still catch up to them!"

Joshua 2:4,5 (Good News Bible)

I watched them go out of the gates with their troops and the gate shut after them.

It was time to have it out with these men, and I said what was on my mind.

"I know that God has given you this land. We're all afraid here. Everyone in the country is terrified if they think they are in your path. We've heard how the Lord dried up the Red Sea when you came out of Egypt and what your armies did to the two kings of the Ammorites just east of here; and how you cursed and then totally destroyed the cities of Sihon and Og. When we knew you were headed towards us here, our hearts sank and our courage left us because we know you have God with you–the God of the heavens above and the earth beneath.

"Now here's the deal. I've done the right thing by you, and now I want you to do the right thing by me. I want a guarantee of life for my father and my mother, my sisters and my brothers, and everyone connected with my family.

Save our lives, and don't let us die."

And Salmon said to me:

"Our life for yours. If you don't tell anyone of our business, we will do the right thing by you and all of your household when God gives us this land."

So, I let them out of the city through my window. They climbed down a rope to the ground.

As they were leaving, I said to Salmon:

"Go into the hills to avoid the King's guards and their troops. Hide there three days until you see the guards return to the gate. Then you'll be safe to return to your people."

Salmon replied:

"I'll keep my word to you. When we come back to the city, tie my scarlet cord to this window we are leaving from. Then get all of your family and everyone connected to your family here into the house. I can't guarantee anyone who leaves the house, but I give you my word to take full responsibility for everyone in the house."

And I said:

"I believe you."

Joshua 2:8-19

Yesterday, the news flew round town that the Israelites moved across the river in one day.

It's impossible, of course.

That river was our city's protection—it's been between us and their army. The news crier called through the streets:

"Joshua, the Israelites' army chief, led the people walking across Jordon River. Their God has done it again, and the water dried up as the soles of the feet of the priest carrying the ark stood in the water at the water's edge so they could walk across the riverbed. The water coming down rose up as a massive wave while every person crossed. Joshua ordered the heads of their twelve tribes to carry twelve stones from the river bed to our side of the river, and they've built a monument at the place where they arrived."

They've closed the city gates, and the city is under siege. It's eerie, unreal as the people inside have taken to the streets and the pubs are full tonight. The latest song at the city tavern today is about them—it's a catchy tune, and I remembered it to tell the girls when I got home:

"When Israel went out of Egypt,

The clan of Jacob left those barbarians behind.
Judah was his sanctuary
And Israel his country to rule.
The sea took one look at them and fled.
The river Jordan was driven back by their power.
The mountains skip like rams
And the little hills like lambs.
What's wrong with you, sea, that you fled
Jordan, that you turned and ran?
What's wrong with you, mountains, that you skip like rams
And you, hills, like spring lambs?"

Tremble Earth, you're in God's presence!
The presence of Jacob's God!
He turned the rock onto a pool of cool water,
From flint into fresh spring waters.

The war started this morning. There's a calm dread through the city, though not a shot has yet been fired.

The armies moved within sight of the city walls yesterday. From the lookout spots on the city wall, we can see them camped to the horizon. We've got a bird's eye view from the windows of our business, and we've been watching them. They work with precision, setting up their tents, moving in supplies, expediting their routines day and night, and there is no stillness about any of their men.

At sunrise today, we heard the sound of trumpets. Everyone who could ran to see what was happening at the camp of our invaders. We saw a procession. First seven priests moved to the head, playing their call to war anthems on trumpets. As they began to move the procession forward, we could see the golden angels and golden ark of their God move forward behind the priests. The army generals began to march in military style and took their position in front of the priests, while their armies took the rear guard behind the ark. The priests trumpeted continually, and we watched in awe as they began to march to the base of the city walls, seven deep, and began circling the city. They wore fighting armor, carrying their weapons, and the town watched these big men, fit from years of being in the desert, well-fed, and strong, and we knew they would not tire in the battle. From our windows and from the city lookout points on the walls, we could see by their faces that they knew their plans. Their purpose is to destroy us, and we know they will do it. As the thousands of soldiers circled the city, they became fourteen deep, then twenty-eight, fifty-six, one hundred and twelve—we lost count. They marched as one, and their heavy boots shook the earth with each step, hour after hour, while their whole army circled the city once.

Inside the city, we hid in terror. The soldiers on the walls didn't want to start a battle they couldn't win so they stood at the ready, tense and frustrated. They waited for the first fire of arrows, the first attempt to ram the gates, but nothing came.

And then, all at once, the march stopped.

The night is dark and quiet.

The city is shut down. No business for us. The army chiefs are locked in for the night: debating the options, determining our future.

As for me and my family, we've determined our future too. The scarlet rope hangs from our window. We're not moving from the house because Mum and I have been putting provisions by for days now. We've thrown in our lot with Salmon and his people.

It has been the same for six days. When the marching starts each day, terror has spread through the streets. Was today the day they would actually attack? How long will the walls hold? There are cracks appearing with the shaking of the ground around the city perimeter day after day, hour after hour. In the last two days, our soldiers sent a volley of arrows down on them, but the Israelites' shields deflect the arrows like annoying flies. Our soldiers stopped, defeated. Not an arrow was fired in return, and not a sound was heard from those thousands of men—not a word. Only the trumpets continuously sound out their songs of war, their songs of the victories of God.

Are they psyching us out?

Or will they starve us out?

Today, they started marching before dawn. The trumpets started, and the beat of the marching echoed and shook through streets and windows throughout the town. From the walls, we can see their faces, and we are all afraid of them. By mid-afternoon, we knew it was different to the other days. They circled once, twice, three times—more. Altogether, those armies circled the city seven times. The streets emptied as everyone barricaded themselves in their homes, and our army held their positions on the top of the walls all around the city. Women in the houses were crying, praying.

And then it sounded like the end of the world as the walls started to crack open, and Joshua called out to his armies.

"Shout, for God has given you the city.

The city and everyone in the city will be destroyed.

Only Rahab the prostitute and the people in her brothel will live because she hid my spies when I sent them to this city. And you, the Armies of Israel, there is to be no looting or stealing anything from the city, because that will bring us trouble in our camp. But bring all of the silver, gold, iron, and brass you find to the tabernacle tent treasury."

Well, that was it!

There's not a soul on our side (or their side) who doesn't know what I am and what I have done.

There could be no turning back, whatever the outcome of the day.

I checked the rope; it was still hanging in the window.

And then we could hear nothing except the crashing of the wall, as it collapsed inwards crushing homes and people as they ran from the walls. We hugged together in our terror, waiting for the falling of our walls. Some of us screamed in fear, screaming and gripping each other as we watched our walls trembling like in an earthquake. And then it was quiet for just a moment–or was it an hour? We heard the army swarm the city but we stayed where we were, locked in our house. We heard the killing of all the men and women, old and young: the sheep, cows, and donkeys. I blocked my ears and closed my eyes so I didn't have to face what was happening and waited for it to be over.

I wanted it to be over.

And then my mother was pulling my hands from my ears and saying to me, "It's Salmon at the door. He's calling you. Go and open the door."

I ran to the door and flew into his arms. I knew I loved him then. And he said:

"Joshua has sent me to get you, and your family, and all who are here with you. Come with me because I have set up tents for all of you just outside our camp. You are safe with us. Joshua has assured me we will keep my promise to you."

We went quickly to the camp of the Israelites. I looked back at the city I had left, which was just rubble on the ground, except for a small tower house that had been our house. The armies were burning the city, and the light of the fires lasted all through the night.

And when it was over, Salmon returned to me, and we were married the same day. I, with all my family and the women who've been part of our business, am starting a new life. I am walking tall and proud and strong, as my family has been accepted as members of our new nation. We are famous and Joshua, our leader, is famous everywhere.

We will build a new future.

A different family business.

Walking Strong

Rahab walked strong from the moment she put two feet on the ground. She grew to maturity in an environment, a profession, that breeds strength to survive.

Her first challenge when she met Salmon was survival; that one she worked out very quickly. She chose life for herself and for her household. Loyalty was an important, non-negotiable value in her house.

The challenge for some of us is to walk strong on a different road.

It was Rahab's second challenge.

That takes courage.

- Courage to challenge the status quo and see the need to change.
- Courage to consider another way of life; one that is foreign to all that you know.
- Courage to be committed and determined to change and to execute it with integrity.
- Courage to tell your family, circle of friends, work team that things need to be different and influence them to take the new road with you.
- Courage to make a move, take the first step.
- Courage to build the new.

We only know that Rahab was successful in starting her walk down a new road through the family tree and their history recorded. Even though she walked strong, she (with her old and new family) faced struggles.

Some hope for the happy-ever-after stories, particularly when it relates to matters of faith and religious (or spiritual) commitments. The grace of God doesn't exempt people from struggles: His grace is the glue that mends the cracks of wear, the broken hearts, the chips of hurt and disappointment. When grace enfolds us, our walk becomes strongly secure for more than a lifetime.

Questions for Reflection

Rahab faced an impossible circumstance. Salmon came into her life to meet her need. Do you think that it's possible these days to span the impossible gap between where you are (or someone you know of is) and where you want to be?

What do you think about Rahab's strategy to save her family?

There are so amazing stories of courageous people in war. Whose stories do you know, and what struck you about their story and their courage?

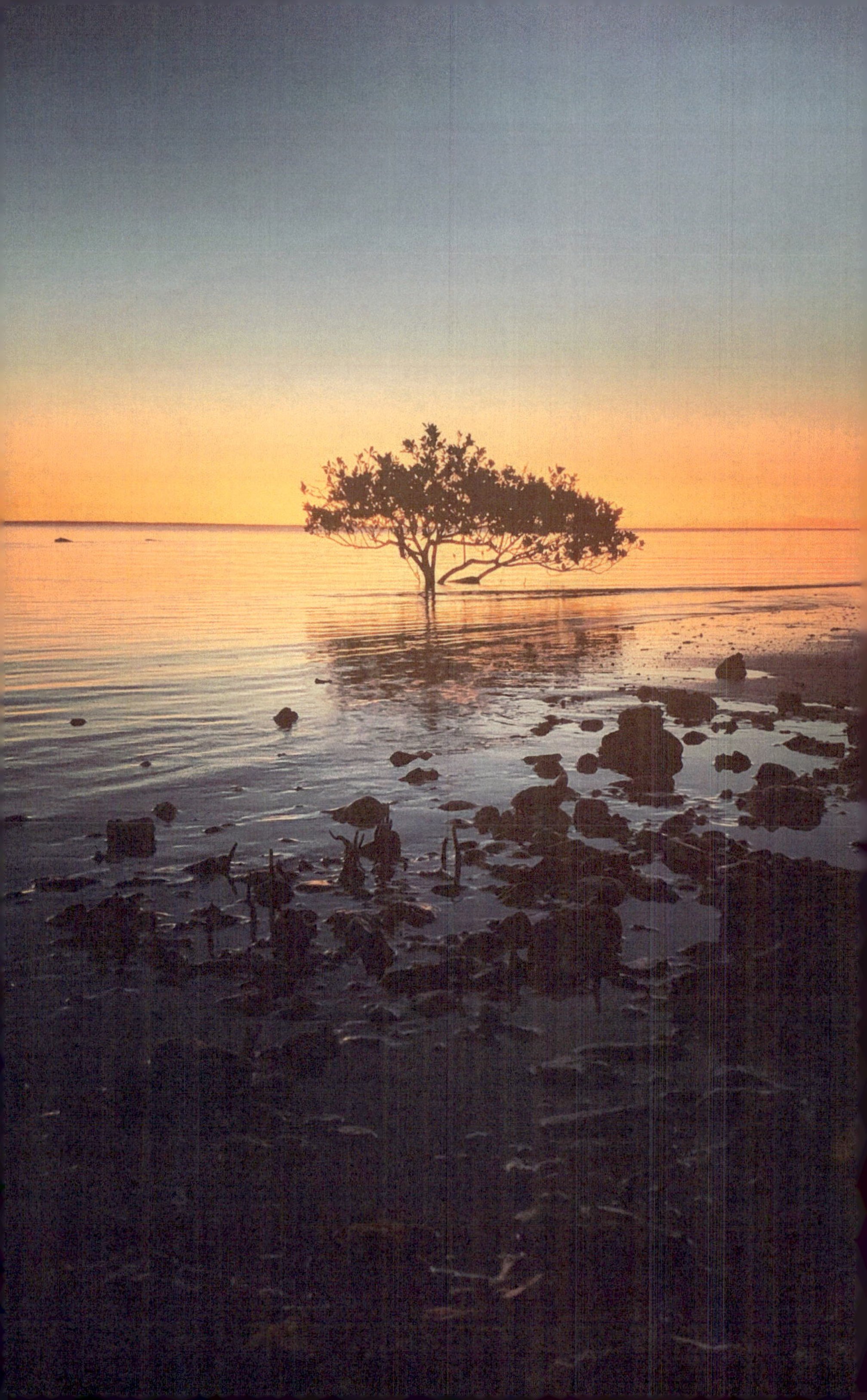

The Divorcee

20s AD

I'm the woman that breaks up marriages.

That's the conversation my group of friends past have when my name comes up.

A couple of the women stay loyal and make sure we catch up–they mean a lot to me.

My life in that group of people is long gone. They are living the life we all hope for as young people–achieving their dreams, accepted everywhere they choose to go.

A few weeks ago, I met my daughter and a friend at a café close to home for dinner. At the table next to them was one of the women from my past group of friends. "Deep breath," I told myself and just say "hello" as you go past the table. Not a chance! I got the "no eye contact treatment," as she was suddenly deep in conversation. Oh well, you just have to get on with life. She'd said a friendly "hello" to my daughter as she arrived–I hated the pointed snub in front of my daughter, especially knowing her friends tell her the gossip about me and ask about it.

I live in a town that doesn't have running water. We rely on two wells. One is close to town on the east side, which most of the women use. I go to the other one—a very old well. I go mid-afternoon when it's the quietest time of day, and I never have to run into any of those people. I just want a quiet life.

Last week, on my way to the well for water, I was enjoying the wave of the fields of the early summer, ready for harvest, and as I got close to the well, I could see this guy sitting beside the well. His dress gave him away as not local (he had fringes on the edge of his garment), from one of our neighbor towns where the people will not ever speak to people from our community.

Oh well, at least it was a stranger.

He looked tired, worn-out.

Safe enough.

"Can you please give me a drink of water?"

I couldn't believe it.

I replied:

"How is it that you are ok to ask me for a drink of water when you know where I live? You people go out of your way to have nothing to do with us."

"If you knew how God wants to give you good gifts and you knew who I was, you would have felt ok to ask me for life water," he said.

He wanted to talk with me! It's been such a long time since that happened to me, and I felt respect from him towards me.

"Sir, you have no bucket to get water from a well as deep as this one, so where would you get life water from? Are you someone who is greater than our ancestor who dug this well for our town?"

He said:

"When you drink this water, you get thirsty again later. I will give you a gift of life water that is never-ending."

"Yep, I'd love you to give me that. I'd never have to come to this well again."

"Okay. Would you like to bring your husband back to share some water with us?"

He was obviously trying to reassure me that he wasn't chatting me up now. That was a good sign. I liked this person–such a normal conversation, for a change.

"Oh, that's okay. I'm not married."

Then he started saying the most amazing things. He said, "I know you've had five husbands, and you haven't married the guy you are with now." He said it kindly–didn't condemn.

I thought to myself, This guy knows I've had a really hard time. Tears were prickling. We talked about my first arranged marriage—I had been reluctant. When I married him, I put my concerns behind and thought we'd build our dreams–children, family.

But foolishly, I fell in love with Matt, a friend, and lived with the long pain of rejection from my family when I divorced and remarried.

This guy at the well knew my pain when Matt left me with a little boy barely walking for someone else. In time, we got back together. The guy at the well understood how I ended up ten years later painfully discovering my husband was a man who needed many affairs, and so I began proceedings to be divorced again–a single mum with two children.

Eddie left his wife to marry me. We started married life full of hope, of dreams, and great support from temple friends to build a good future. Did I realize he was an abusive man before we got married? Years later, my kids told me they knew. I knew I had to get out eventually when that unhappiness affected first one, then both my kids. I had to reduce the risk that my daughter would be a statistic in an abusive relationship of her own.

This guy at the well, he understood.

Then there was Joe, who I married then shared the last months of his life. I've never regretted those weeks of friendship, laughter, and tears.

Ten years alone.

These days, I have a lover. A group of girls talked once about finding a Mr. Wednesday. He brings fruit and cooks dinner on Wednesday night. He goes home Thursday morning. A perfect match, we laughed.

I found one.

He's a good man, and we don't talk about getting married.

Been there, done that.

I don't think about future. One day at a time.

This guy at the well did not condemn, but it was obvious that He is a really good man–as perfect as I imagine a person could be.

He's not at all like me.

He had my utmost respect.

He was talking with me and treating me with honor, knowing I was making a huge effort to live peacefully, looking after my family and friends.

I could feel tears prickling my eyes again.

Kindness is sometimes hard to take.

I needed a bit of personal space and took the conversation to safer ground.

"Sir, I know you are a holy person. You know we have our temple on the mountain outside the city–you can see it way up there behind you, built by our ancestors. But the people in your town say the only legitimate temple is the one your ancestors built. What do you say?"

"Dear lady, in a very short time, it won't matter where people worship. The people in your temple don't know what or who they are worshipping; whereas my people do know who God is. Very soon, though, people will worship God the Father in Spirit and in truth and these are the kind of worshippers that God is looking for."

John 4:21 The Message

I knew what He was talking about. His words were plain and simple.

"Yes," I said. "When the Jewish Messiah comes, the Christ, he will tell us how to worship like this."

"I'm Him. You're speaking to the Christ."

Then I noticed His group of friends had arrived from town where they had obviously gone to buy food, but when they got back from town, they hadn't interrupted us.

I left my bucket for them and went home.

I met people all the way back–their afternoon trip to get their evening water. I couldn't stay quiet.

"When you get to the well, you'll see this guy who is the Jewish Messiah. I'm certain because He could tell me about everything that has happened to me, even though He has never been here before."

Can you believe it? A lot of those people went and talked to Him, and He ended up stayed in town for two days. In those days, He talked, and we heard the deepest and purest truths. It was wonderful! And many more people in town now believe that He is the Christ, the Messiah.

On one of those days, He said to me, "This is a poem that I know is true about you." He read out:

"You [God] created every part of me
You put me together in my mother's womb
I praise you because I am in awe of you
All you do is strange and wonderful
I know it with all my heart.
When my bones were being formed
Carefully put together in my mother's womb
When I was growing there in secret
You [God} knew that I was there
You saw me before I was born.
The number of days that I will live are written in your book of all things
Before any of those days began."

Extract from the Good News Bible Psalm 139 v13-16

Then He added,

"Even your fingerprints have been uniquely created and each imprint you make on the world is unique and can only be made by you."

How amazing!

My friends say that I brought important news to town. What I know is that He thought I was worth talking to, and He gave me confidence to choose to be the person I'd like to be.

And more amazing still, I've since found out that I was the first person who He actually told straight out that He is our Messiah!

He chose me to introduce Him to this town.

How does that happen?

Some of the people in town have said to me, "We believe that Jesus is the Messiah. Not because you told us, but because we talked to Him for ourselves."

Just goes to show, doesn't it, that when people decide to choose God, they don't necessarily choose to be gracious and kind.

Walking Strong

Life feels a bit easier at the moment. I can do each day in a peaceful way, knowing that I'm valued as a person.

I can pray anytime and talk with God.

He doesn't condemn me, and I'm working through a mountain of stuff as time goes on. He doesn't drop me in my weakness or say He'll be my friend when I've got myself sorted out and on the right track.

My friends are gold. I'm realizing that there is always going to be a friend to support me and encourage me who shares this faith that I have. I know more about how to recognize friends who are godly–the real deal.

Friends never condemn. They don't condone, but they never judge.

Friends seek you out and stand by you through the rough as well as the fair weather.

Friends give you hope for the future.

Friends show kindness in every circumstance.

Meeting the guy at the well showed me who God is. He cared enough to show Himself to me.

Now I understand grace–kindness freely given. No strings attached.

It's an amazing thing. He chose me to be His friend.

I've seen Him.

I've sat and talked with God.

Questions for Reflection

People who have been bruised and wounded are fragile. God is the friend of the wounded heart and has a place for the bruised and weary.

How do you handle people in this circumstance?

What do you say?

Recall a time when you were heartbroken. How did you respond? How long did it take to recover?

What sorts of things help so that a broken person can recover?

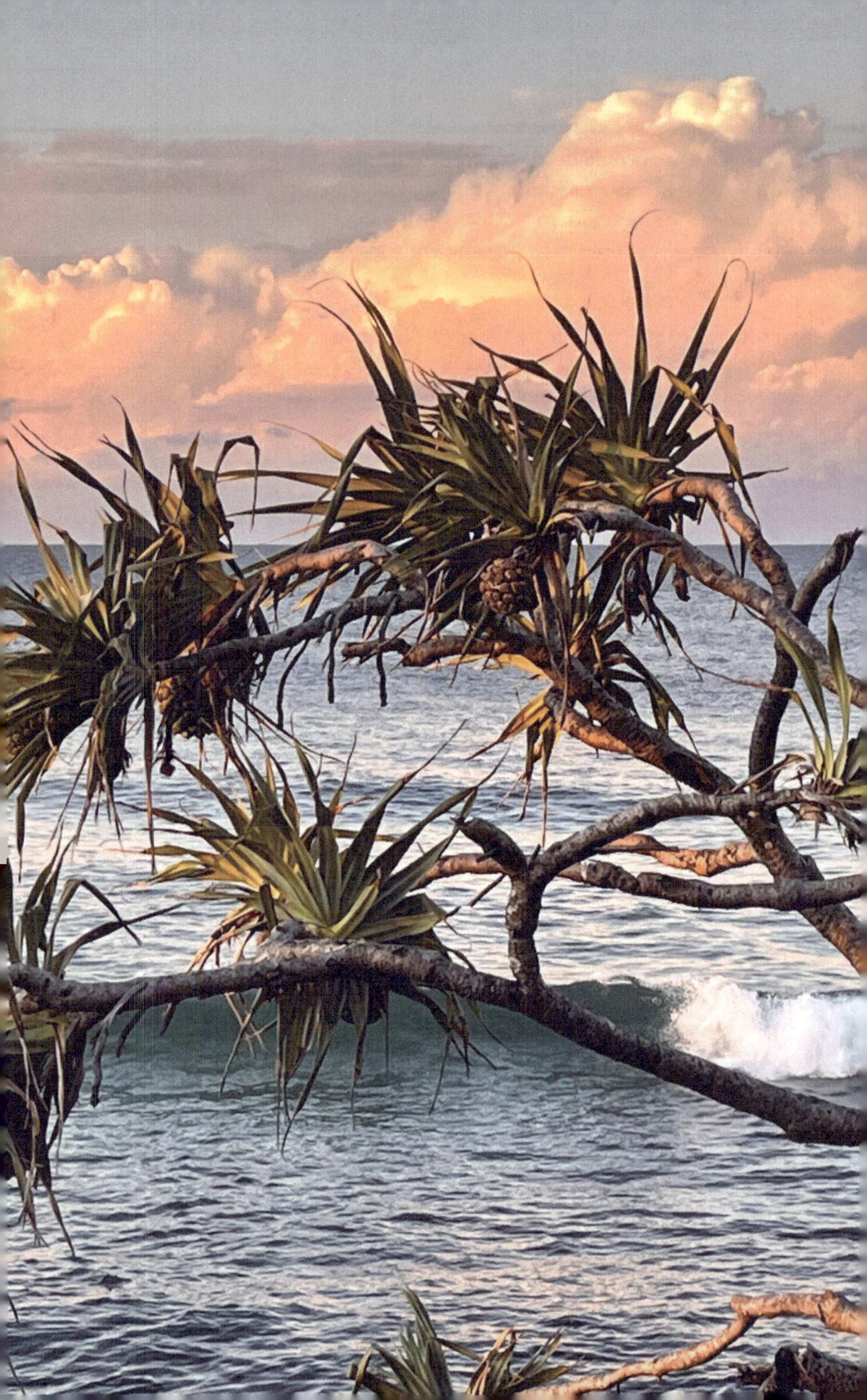

Eve

Sixth day of Creation

My Father's eyes were the first thing I ever saw.
His eyes adored me.
He loved me from the moment I drew breath.
And I adored Him. I worshipped Him.
He'd made for me a perfect world, a perfect mate, a perfect life.
Every day was exciting and full; and time had no meaning.
Adam and I were so full of love and excitement about the world we could build with our Father.
We worked hard and played hard.
We watched the seasons come and go, enjoying the cycle of our food harvests.
We were in awe of the weather and its patterns, its ferocity and those wonderful perfect days.
We were absorbed in the complexity of all of the animals on land and in the sea, and we watched the day to day of their lives. We came to understand their patterns for life and the ways in which they intertwined with ours.
We husbanded those animals, domesticated to support us with eggs and milk.
We explored the world and all the extravagance, beauty, and grandeur of nature.

- Feeling tiny standing beneath towering thundering waterfalls, or floating over brilliant reef gardens teeming with fish flashing shapes and colours, or standing at the edge of great canyons weathered by water and wind.
- Breathtaking landscapes of desert, never-ending and forever-changing, mountains high and wild, valleys winding, plains as far as the eye can see, islands, forests, rivers, oceans, and ice lands—each place unique and made for our pleasure.
- The challenges and tiredness of a day's work lifted from my shoulders, as I wriggled my feet in soft sand, put my face to the salt spray blown by the breeze toward me, and listened to the endless lullaby of the waves on the seashore.

- Feeling and smelling soft new grass just dry from the morning dew in paddocks on the hillside, or snowflakes falling softly in the silent spaces of unmarked snow, stretching far beyond my eye's sight.
- Sounds of birds in musical symphonies to herald the dawn or relaxing songs at dusk, as we wind down for the evening.
- The excitement of discovering the smallest worlds of tiny insects and plants. Sitting still, day after day, until we had identified everything in these miniature ecosystems. Their daily habits, their sounds, their colours, their territories, their life cycles.

Together
We played
Worked
Enjoyed exquisite food
Made love–a lot
Rested.
And the conversation!
Every evening, we walked in the garden with God, our Father.
We laughed and debated and puzzled things out.
Shared deeply.
We looked at life, and it was good.
His wisdom was as wide as it was deep, and we learned wisdom.
We built plans and made them happen.

God loved surprises as much as we did. We tried out new ideas, made presents, engineered our home—I loved to see my Father thrilled and see how proud He was of me.

Life with Adam was so much fun—marriage was perfect. We worked together, talked about our future together, talked about making a family together.

Every day, we laughed. Just imagine the jokes. (Oh, you have!)

Adam thought he'd play a joke on Eve. He walked up to her with a cucumber up his nose, a banana in one ear, and a carrot in the other ear.
"What's wrong with me?" he asked.
Eve replied, "You're not eating properly,"

Adam and Eve were walking across broad plains they had not seen before and came across a hole in the ground.
"I wonder how deep it is?" said Eve.

Adam picked up a rock that was laying nearby and let it drop. They listened and listened but did not hear it hit the bottom.

Eve said, "Adam, help me get this big log over, and we'll see if we can hear when it hits the bottom."

They dragged the log to the edge and as they tipped it up, it fell fast. They listened, but they heard nothing at all. Adam turned away from the hole and saw a massive goat galloping toward them, fierce in the face and snorting wildly as it got closer. Adam grabbed Eve and pushed her to the side just in time as the goat went down the hole. They leaned over the side and listened but did not hear it hit the bottom.

And then they saw God walking over the ridge, and He walked until He reached them.

"Have you seen my goat?" He said.

"Yes, he was a fierce and angry goat, and he charged down the hill at us. We just got out of the way or he would have hurt us," replied Eve.

"Oh, not that one," said God. "I mean the nice, quiet one that I tied to the log out here yesterday."

"How do you get down off an elephant?
You don't, you get down off a duck."

****

And we worshipped.

Can you imagine what it is like to sing with angels? They filled the skies and sang–all kinds of music: all the music of the earth and the music of the heavens.

We heard them, and we rushed to join them.

We sang our hearts out.

We made our own songs to worship our amazing God.

Wonderful.

Counsellor.

Our everlasting Father.

The Mighty God.

The Prince of Peace.

We watched fantastic light shows.

All of Creation showed the majesty of God. We saw it in the lightening and the thunder of the clouds. We saw it in the Northern Lights of the Arctic and the Southern Lights of the Antarctic, and we saw it in the still, small whisper of a breeze.

Our faces shone with the glory of His presence throughout our worship.

It's overwhelming to be in His presence. We fell down before Him and cried, "Holy, holy is the Lord."

It's overwhelming to worship knowing you were made because God wanted the company of people.

People made in His own image.

His eyes adored us.

All my life, I will remember how warm and tender we were together.

****

How do you find meaning when you've lost a perfect life?

Our stunned shock became grief, knowing we could not go back to the garden.

Some years after that were so full of sadness and regret—getting through the day felt like wading through treacle.

My memories are strong of our beginning life, and they have a terrible kind of beauty that comes from being reduced to nothing more than the present moment.

You can remember those times—but you can't change that you've lost them.

And then the dawning of knowing there is a life to be lived.

There was satisfaction in seeing the fruit of our labors. We continued to farm the land after we left the garden. I love caring for the earth. My passion through the years has been in storing food after harvest for the other seasons.

We still love design as we learned from our Father. It's very satisfying to build farming tools as well as fitting out and furnishing our home.

However, I miss the daily walks with our Father.

We still talk a lot.

Joy returned with the birth of our children–our beautiful boys and girls.

When each little person was born, they were perfect. Their innocence was a treasure to hold and to remember.

Of course, perfection in my babies could not last.

Oh, how I hate the fighting and the jealousies and the lies.

Why did I think that part of life would broaden our understanding?

It has constrained our relationships and caused painful hurts.

I could never have imagined it.

If I had been able to imagine it, I'd never have chosen it.

Why would anyone choose something that wasn't a perfect life?

But there's the truth.

We were given the choice—and it was with us always and forever.

And we, knowing God in a perfect world, could choose to know imperfection.

We, together, decided to try imperfection.

It cost our life.

We broke our Father's heart.

Our Father, in His sadness, did what only He could do. He made a blood sacrifice for us to atone for our wrongdoing.

I wept to see that innocent creature die.

I was shocked to see the blood spill.

My Father took the skin of that animal and gave them to Adam and I so that we were not naked.

Our Father, in His sadness, promised to my family, and all who follow, that there will come a time when He will raise a person up to repair the consequences of our wrongdoing, our poor choice; and there will come a time when He will restore our perfect world and share this world with everyone who chooses Him.

I choose Him.

I long to live again in His presence. This is my hope and my future.

I know His love for me is forever.

Our children and our children's children are made in our image and in the image of God.

They have a choice.

They can choose to know God in an imperfect world.

My heart aches for those who don't choose God, especially for Cain. He lives with the pain of causing a person's death, the taking of a life.

I'm his mother. I love him.

We know what death is like now.

How can parents endure such grief that comes with the death of their child? Our beautiful son Abel became a man and was gone suddenly from us.

Killed violently by his brother.

I wept that one of my precious children would experience death—Adam's and my legacy to our children.

It was shocking to face that day and the days after—shocking to put my dear child in the grave.

We did not wish our child to perish and still be here ourselves!

I could not look at the depth of sadness in Adam's face. Our sorrow was so

deep, we could not console each other.
We each felt so alone in our mourning.
Since Eden, that has been the hardest thing that has ever happened to me. For a long time, I lost my life.
I just did routine, every day. I didn't want to be with Adam, and he couldn't bear to be with me. We just went on.
I wasn't interested in anything;
I didn't want to do anything;
I was just existing.
I didn't want to have to continue making life happen.
And then I thought to myself,
Abel wouldn't have wanted me to live like this.
And so, I started to get on with my life again. It was hard, but I got there eventually.

Walking Strong

After that, I taught my children and grandchildren the ways of God with passion. From their earliest days, I sang God to them and told them of His love and our life in the garden. I told of His grace and desire to give us a wonderful life. Over the years, there were so many children. Some of my children chose God, and my heart filled with gladness to see them grow in faith. Seth was one—he was my gift from God. When he was born, I said to Adam:
"God has granted me another child in place of Abel."

Genesis 4:25 NIV

Having Seth helped Adam and I rebuild our life.
I waited a long time for Enoch, my great, great, great, great-grandchild. We lived so long, you see. But I was there when Enoch was born—he was born to us through Seth's family line.
From his first baby words, he knew God.
How we loved time with him, Adam and I, telling him about our life with God, talking to God together. He lived life as it was meant to be—he was focused on living as we did in the garden—as a friend and companion of God. Throughout his childhood and as an adult, we all said of him, "Enoch walks with God."
How I am thrilled at the sound of his steps at my door.
I know he will walk with God through eternity.

Questions for Reflection

The photos in this book are one person's appreciation of God's creation.

Which of God's creations amaze you?

What does creation communicate about the character of God?

Losing everything is so very tough. It happened to Jesus in the Garden of Gethsemane. In these kinds of struggles, how should we change our strategy?

Eve was the first mother.

As a mother, how do we become the person we want our children to be?

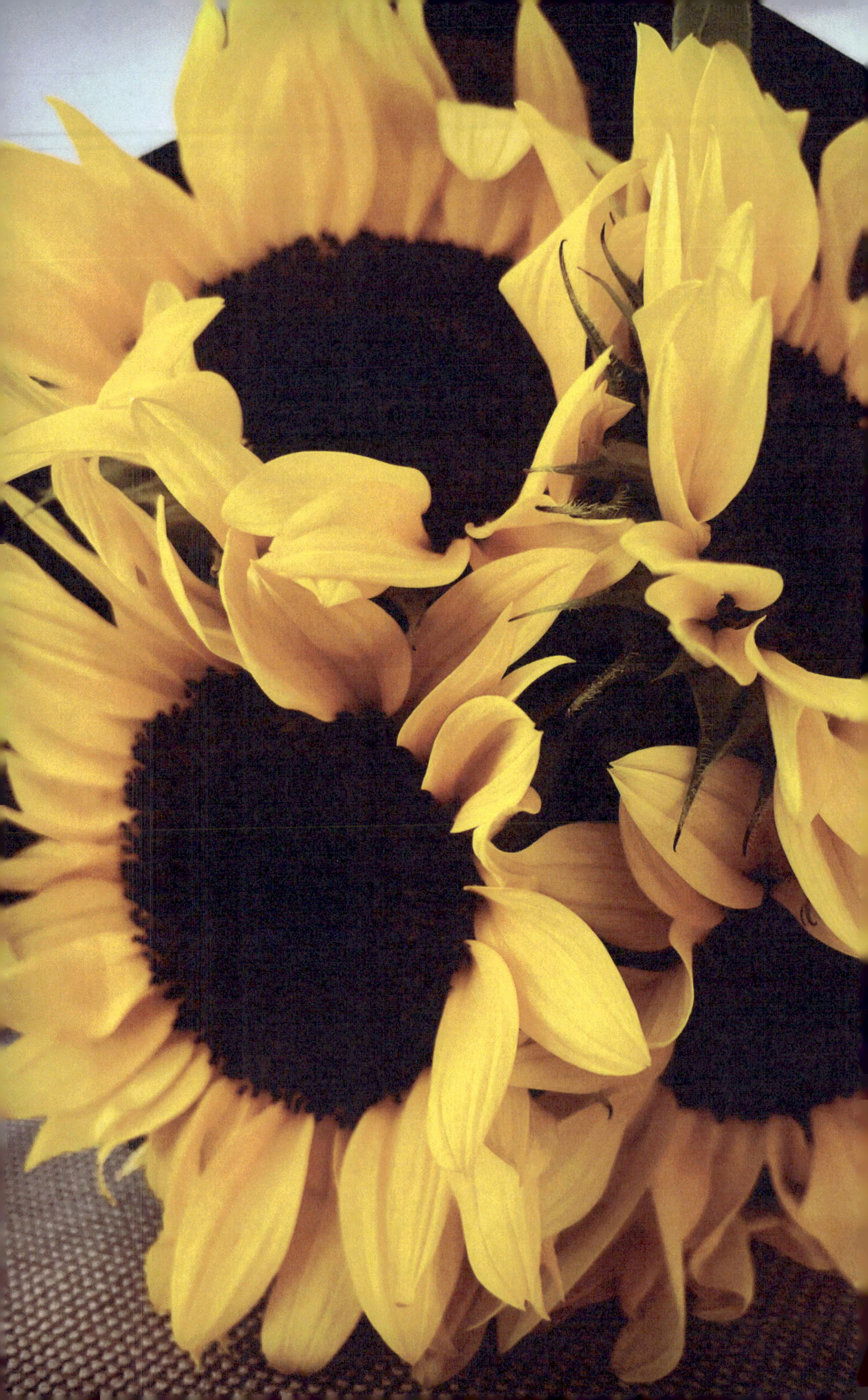

Elizabeth

7 BC

"She asked me how I got pregnant too!"

She laughed as she poured my coffee. We had been talking for some hours now, and I had just said,

"Tell me about Elizabeth."

"Elizabeth was my grandmother's cousin, but when I went to stay with her after the angel spoke to me, she became more like my sister. Those few months– I've never laughed so much in all my life. She was a wonderful, funny person–so full of life, and yet she was an old lady who had never had a baby.

"She and Zachariah both came from the family of Aaron and were so well suited. Zachariah followed the family profession and became a priest. Elizabeth was the daughter of a priest. They were full of hope and excitement starting married life together–he was so committed to his work and married life, and she was such fun; they made a popular couple. In faith, they believed they'd have the blessing of a big family. They were well- known and respected. And as the years went on, Elizabeth had days when she felt desperate about not falling pregnant, really struggling not being jealous of the women around her having babies.

"She got really involved in the community and you know, I joined her a few times when we had that time together. When we walked into the places where the groups met that she worked and lived with, her presence lit up everyone's face straight away. She was just one of those bright and cheeky people.

"One day, she and Zachariah went to visit good friends who had just had their first baby. Elizabeth thought he was so cute! She talked about him all the way home, eyes glowing and when they got inside and sat down for their evening coffee, Zachariah remarked that they must have seen different babies because he saw a baby wrinkled up like the last bunch of dates in the basket. He thought babies looked old! Elizabeth looked at him in disbelief, so he added that the little, toothless terror would probably turn out all right in the end.

"Elizabeth decided, in her heart, that if she couldn't have children, she would accept it. She would not acquire pets who would live inside their home and become her spoiled 'babies'; she would not pick up eccentric hobbies like ornamental Roman gardens replacing their vegetable plot, and she would not go slightly mad and talk to the other women about obscure topics at dinner parties. And she would not listen to well-meaning people that told her there are many other things that could make life whole and meaningful–she told me she used to think to herself things like, They haven't seen my embroidery.

"Zachariah told me one evening that Elizabeth often asked him if he really wanted children. He tried to train their milking goat to nod when she asked. One day, he told her that he thought God had made him to want a whole lot of things, not just the need to reproduce himself. She got a bit pompous and offended for a little while, but that collapsed when Zachariah got his sleeve caught under the goat's foot, and they stumbled until both tumbled in a heap. She could only laugh for the rest of the evening amid his complaints.

"Elizabeth had so many stories of things she tried to get pregnant. We laughed until we cried, Luke, but you're a man, and I can't tell you those stories, even though you are a doctor." She laughed again. "Elizabeth brought such a lot of fun to my life in that time when I needed it most. Oh, the things we laughed about!"

My mind went back to our teacher in fertility at our school of healing, and I smiled.

This teacher was a collector of fertility icons, and they had fascinated us–professionally, of course. He taught us, using a number of case studies. I still laugh to think of his lessons–he was an actor when he told a story.

Some couples believed that if they abstained from sex for weeks, the man would be more potent. The results seemed to suggest it could really spice up the sex life for some couples, though some of the husbands experienced "stage fright" when the time finally arrived. Our teacher thought it was useless as a means to conceive.

One couple had been of the viewpoint that pregnancy was an unknowable, unpredictable lottery, and they pursued having sex all the time–that meant every night and some afternoon delights. The husband outlasted his wife, but they both became exhausted instead of pregnant.

Then there were all the wacky fertility myths he told us about–herbal tea, crystals, ancient rites like making symbols with thumb and forefinger and chanting words like "flow," aromas like rose and geranium oils, fennel and ginger (which stinks), nutmeg oil massages, and fertility ceremonies.

There was one fertility story that had us all rolling in the aisles of the lecture forum. One couple had performed their fertility ceremony on top of a local hillside under a full moon—candles and perfumed Ood, especially bought from an Arabian Bedouin, burning in an incense holder. A passing family going home from a friend's birthday celebration, which had gone on late into the evening, surprised them. In their haste to hide and cover themselves, the husband threw on his robes, only to feel a large lizard run up his back. His wife watched him galloping down the hill in the moonlight, trying to rid himself of the thing.

Mary was talking again.

"Elizabeth told me over the years they heard all the stories.

Couples who had given up hope only to have four children in three years! Someone who waited decades and then couldn't stop.

There was one husband who had been a eunuch and produced offspring.

Her cousin told her it was all in the mind; any woman could have a baby.

One of the neighbors told her she was trying too hard and just needed to relax.

A new friend suggested they 'go on a holiday and put it out of your mind and it will just happen.'

She knows them all.

"One day, she even overheard two people chatting about their childless marriage, and one commented, 'Zachariah should divorce her and take another wife. We all need children to keep us young, support us in our old age, keep our name going, give us grandchildren to spoil, show to the world that God has rewarded us for our faithfulness. That would solve his problem of an heir.'

When she'd relayed that to Zachariah, his response was, 'I have known of many who marry fine women, only to find they are given to an overly sharp tongue and scathing wit. In their own homes, they are ordered about and find their nerves are bad. There are far greater risks than not having children in marriage. One man I know only sees his wife on prescribed holidays and tries to spend the rest of his time at their beach house!–Not like us.' He chased her round and round the kitchen table, and they laughed breathlessly 'til they were both caught.

"After that, she held her head high in the face of cultural disgrace.

She would not be morbid. She purposefully worked towards being the best she could be. She was an expert in many areas of her interests and was respected amongst her peers.

"Their friends' children grew up, and Elizabeth and Zachariah missed out on the first day at school for the boys, music lessons and sports days, mothers having the company at home of their girls in daily baking and mending, market days, family celebrations like the boys' bar mitzvahs when they turned thirteen, and the negotiations and excited planning of weddings. They went to lots of weddings of their friends' children.

"And still, they prayed and hoped for a child of their own.

"As they reached grandparenting age, Elizabeth was determined not to miss out. There were two young couples whose parents had died due to illness, and Elizabeth and Zachariah took the couples under their wings. They were perfect for those families, each providing nurture and comfort and support to the other.

"Zachariah was a devil with the children in those families. Often, he would tease them and then chase them. Elizabeth would hear them squealing as they tore out of the house to hide. He always found them and 'rumbled them' to the ground, covering their faces and arms with ticklish kisses. They called him 'monster' and adored him. He would read them a story and when it got to the most exciting part, he'd tell them he'd finish it the next time they visited. Other times, he would sneak them extra sweets when their mothers said they'd had enough, and the little ones would fall asleep in his arms with his beard tickling their noses. Those kids would chat to Elizabeth and Zachariah about all sorts of things that were news to the parents—they wanted to be kind and generous to each person in every circumstance."

Mary paused.

"They were like that to me at our family get-togethers on special occasions.

"Elizabeth told me that this was a very happy time. She was content with life, and Zachariah felt fulfilled in life—their marriage and his work were good."

Mary stopped, seeing that I was still writing madly, but I said, "Go on. Please keep going."

"Then I saw the angel one day. He appeared in front of me and told me his name was Gabriel. It was amazing that such an important angel would visit me and talk to me–and he knew my name! He told me that I would have Jesus and that I would become pregnant, even though I was a virgin. I couldn't really understand it (though I remember every word) so he told me that Elizabeth was six months pregnant. For me, that was a miracle!

And then he waited for me to answer.

I was very honored and said 'yes' willingly.

I was so excited that the Messiah was coming.

I thought everyone would be thrilled with me.

I was very young.

"And just like that, I was pregnant.

My parents didn't know what to do when I told them. They wanted to believe me, but struggled. My mother paced the floor and cried. My dad would not look at me and could not eat; he was trying to think of what to do.

Then we all thought of Joseph, my fiancée–telling him was a multitude of problems!

I wished I could see Elizabeth.

And with that thought, I decided to go to her straight away that same day. I couldn't wait to talk to her about–well, everything.

"My dad took me because it was a few days' walk from our place to theirs.

We could not let them know I was coming so I wasn't sure she was at home when we finally got to their little town in the hill country of Judea. When we saw their house, I ran inside, calling out to Elizabeth. She gave a glad cry as she turned to see me.

"And then she exclaimed,

'God has blessed you above all women, and your child is blessed.

Why am I so honored that the mother of my Lord should visit me? When I heard your greeting, the baby in my womb jumped for joy. You are blessed because you believed that the Lord would do what he said.'

"How did she know?

I stopped in my tracks.

Dad stood at the door; his jaw dropped in shock.

Her face was shining.

'Oh, Mary, when I heard your call, my baby leaped inside me and the Spirit of God filled me, and I knew straight away your wonderful news.'"

Luke 1:44

Mary paused.

"You know, Luke, I realized then that the Spirit was God was in me also, and He gave me the most wonderful words to say in reply.

It was my own personal worship and praise.

Do you remember? We talked about it the first day we met."

I looked back through my notes.

"Mary, I wrote it out just as you remembered it, because it is such a beautiful song of praise. I want to publish it in the record I am writing if it's okay with you."

She nodded, still thinking about Elizabeth.

"Elizabeth hugged us both–Dad and me, and then made lunch for us. We both cheered up and chatted and laughed over lunch about the chickens not laying, and she'd been out that morning shaking the cleaver at them. She also asked if I could stay for about three months–I was so happy because then I might be there when her baby was born, and Dad was happy to agree. He headed off the next morning back home and made sure I knew he believed me before he left. That was a big relief.

"We spent the next day talking about how blessed we were and how wonderful our babies' lives were going to be. I told Elizabeth about the angel, Gabriel, appearing in front of me and about what he had. She was amazed that I had a virgin pregnancy. And she said,

'Mary, Zachariah and I have been ardent students and believers of the promised Messiah all our married lives. Thinking about it now, it shouldn't be all that surprising because it is one of Isaiah's prophesies. Let's find it.'

And we did. I realized that over the years, Zachariah had taught Elizabeth to read and write, and she showed me their Torah parchments.

My eyes opened wider while she read the words in their parchment of Isaiah in the seventh chapter:

'Therefore, the Lord himself will give you a sign; The virgin will be with child and will give birth to a son, and will call him Immanuel' which means 'God with us.'

"Elizabeth told me their story too.

They had become very old. A childless, old couple.

Her only concession over the years about being barren had been to be sad that she could not hope that their child might possibly be the Messiah. Lots of her friends hoped their child would grow up to be the Messiah. And then the strangest thing happened to Zachariah.

"Zachariah wasn't a senior priest–but he belonged to one of the twenty-four groups that did priestly service in the Temple in Jerusalem. He had an honorable place and each year served for two weeks at the Temple where about fifty were rostered each day, and the daily team of priests drew lots for the functions they would undertake on the day. During these times, he and Elizabeth stayed with friends who lived close by to the Temple.

"At the time of this day's morning sacrifice, the massive Temple gates would have swung slowly open on their hinges, and a three-fold blast from the silver trumpets of the priests would have woken the city to the life of another day.

"On this day, as the trumpets echoed through the streets, Elizabeth's thoughts wandered through the chain of promises of the present, past, and future that bound the Holy City of Jerusalem to their souls.

"On that bright autumn morning, Zachariah, already at the Temple, had no such thoughts. For the first, and for the last time in his life, his lot was for incensing, and every thought would have centered on the proper performance of this office.

It was an honor.

First, he had to choose two of his friends or relatives to assist in his sacred service. One had to reverently remove what had been left on the altar from the previous evening's service. The second, in worship, spread live coals from the sacrificial fire of offerings to the verge of the golden altar. They did that without incident.

Then, as the music heralding the innermost part of worship of the day sounded out beyond the precincts of the city, Zachariah waited alone in the inner room for the special signal. When it sounded, he spread the incense on the altar as close as possible to the place called the Holy of Holies. He knew all the people were waiting outside, bowed prostrate in silence, watching for the symbol of their prayers of incense rising toward heaven. When he saw the incense kindle, he made a bow and withdraw from the room in worship, but he saw an angelic form on the right side of the altar, and his movement stopped, arrested. This had never happened in the history of the nation–a vision to an ordinary priest in the act of incensing.

It was the angel Gabriel, speaking to him.

The angel reminded him of his lifelong prayers and hopes which by now had passed into the background of his memories. He told him that he and Elizabeth would have a child, and the child would be a great man of God. Zachariah felt overwhelmed in his aging, hearing the angel's words, and he scarcely realized their meaning. His voice faltered, saying:

'How can I be sure this will happen? I'm an old man now, and my wife is also well along in years.'

The angel told him to be silent, and that his silence would remain until the child was born.

"And he was struck dumb from that moment.

"He fled the inner sanctuary and was faced with all those people, wondering why he had taken so long to come out after the incense had risen and the sky above was clear again. He should have led the priestly benediction so that the meat offering, song of psalms, and drink offering could be made. He tried to speak, but had no voice. He gestured to what had happened, and the people understood from his actions that he had seen a vision.

"He repeated the same gestures to Elizabeth when he got home. She was amazed!

Zachariah knew that he had to start making a baby. Can you imagine the conversation–his miming and Elizabeth's reactions?"

Mary laughed, a cheeky glint in her eye.

"Elizabeth told me that she'd said to her friend the next day, 'He got that look in his eye last night–and he hasn't had that look for years. Lord, help me!'

"Elizabeth kept very quiet about her pregnancy, nearly until the day that I arrived.

Of course, Zachariah was very quiet too!"

She laughed again, and I looked up. There was merriment in her eyes, and it made us both laugh to think of the poor man, any man for that matter, struck dumb like that. That angel had a wicked sense of humor.

"The next few months with the both of them were great. Zachariah accepted his lot with grace. We shared the excitement and worries of pregnancy. Elizabeth didn't know of anyone else who had had their first baby when they were so old (except our nation's history of Sarah). She didn't want to die, which happens quite often in childbirth. She wanted the joy of rearing her child, though it was unlikely she could live to see him a fully mature man.

She worried about that.

"We also talked about the promises that Gabriel had given to me and to Zachariah. We talked long into the evenings about that. Elizabeth's baby would bring joy and gladness to a far wider circle than that of their family; he would be great before the Lord. He would be a Nazarene (never touching wine or other alcoholic drinks) like Samson and Samuel, wholly belonging to God from his inception, through life and in his work. He would be filled with the Holy Spirit for his lifework from the moment life awoke him. He would be strong and turn many of the people back to a faith in God, having the spirit and power of Elijah.

Our babies would grow up knowing each other well.

We would do everything we could to prepare them for the life that lay ahead of each one.

"The weeks went by so quickly.

It was time for me to go home, but then Elizabeth went into labor. Zachariah couldn't get the midwife there quick enough. It was a difficult labor—her body was old. I stayed by her side.

And then his cry pierced the stillness of the night air.

And he was in his mother's arms and Zachariah beside them.

The baby and mother looked at each other.

His eyes, large and dark in the little face, held his mother's eyes fast. He had a 'wise oldness' look about him—the 'old' face of the babe looking at the 'old' face of the mother. We burst out laughing.

It was with joy.

Zachariah could not take his eyes off his own son. He loved and adored this little babe from the moment he saw him."

She was smiling; remembering; tears in her eyes.

I interrupted her thoughts.

"Mary, did Elizabeth see her son's ministry life? Did she worry when he went to prison?"

"No. She died when he was in his teens. She had wonderful times being a mother, though.

"Elizabeth was quite frail after his birth.

She was telling everyone his name was John, and they insisted that he should be called Zachariah, after his father. Of course, his father couldn't speak, and they seemed to ignore his gestures.

When John was eight days old, the whole town came for his circumcision ceremony. They started to call him Zachariah, but Elizabeth said very firmly, 'No! His name is John.' They looked to Zachariah and raised their hands in question and frustration. Zachariah asked for a writing tablet and wrote in large letters for them all to see 'His name is John.'"

"And then Zachariah was filled with the Spirit of God, and he spoke a prophesy about the person John would become and the impact he would have on them all. And everyone was in awe and spread the news through all the local towns that this baby and this family had the hand of the Lord upon them in a very special way.

"They loved that boy and prepared him well for his future. I learned such a lot from them both. From the very early years and in school breaks, Zachariah took him camping in the surrounding areas, and they became good survivors. John was a great kid, but never happier than those times learning from his dad. She was a wonderful mother. She walked strong–she had walked strong for many years. She encouraged him in everything. And she and I made sure our boys spent lots of time together as they were growing up. She especially loved those times she and Zachariah would teach him the scriptures that he would need later, particularly the prophesies about Jesus, and especially about Elijah; the kind of person he was and how he thought.

"It was an unusual upbringing though–being a Nazarene and preferring desert life to running around town with the other young lads. He spent a lot of time alone when he went out to the desert, surviving on the land.

"Can you imagine the women at the markets? One used to say, 'Poor Elizabeth, she waited so long for a child, and now she's got a weird one.'

"After his parents died, he pretty much lived full time in the desert until he started his lifework, preparing the people for my son's public life and death."

I looked at Mary.

She had stopped talking.

"Tell me about when you went home from Elizabeth and Zachariah's home to your parents and how Joseph managed."

"By the time I got home, I was looking very pregnant. Mum burst into tears as soon as she saw me, and Dad started patting her arm and saying, 'It will be all right. It will be all right.'

But that's another story."

Walking Strong

How does a woman walk strong throughout a lifetime of infertility?

Living well while facing an ongoing, confounding, and confronting issue is difficult, whether it is the context of a personal life, being a leader, working or managing a community group or a multimillion-dollar business. The skills to survive and then thrive are the same. They are:

- Having a clear purpose by developing your personal fields of fascination or goals into decent, lasting lifework and being the best that you can be.
- Integrity in treating every person with respect and having a set of values that works towards everyone in your circle, and affected by your circle, being better off.
- Courage to be authentic, living out values every day, committed to addressing needs when things need to change, and believing in others' judgments.
- Genuine care for the others to give encouragement, be generous and go the extra mile, and support so they can flourish.

Elizabeth walked strongly in her faith. So strongly that she was the first person to refer to Jesus (while He was still in the womb) as Lord, the same word translated as "Lord God," "Yahweh." She was saying, in effect, "Here is the Lord

God, [shortly to be] walking upon the earth." She initiated a chain of events through the expression of these words. I believe she talked about that often to John as the two boys spent time together throughout their childhoods.

Elizabeth was a gracious woman, a chosen personal attribute. That is, she understood grace and showed grace. We know that, from his earliest years, the grace of the Spirit appeared in John's ways.

She was an excellent role model.

Questions for Reflection

Elizabeth, though she lived a lifetime as an infertile woman, was perfectly prepared to support a young pregnant Mary and to be the kind of mother John needed to prepare him for his adult life calling.

Do you agree?

Some couples think they should be fruitful, and some people think they should be "fruitful." Look at John 15:1-3 where there is a discussion about what is important for the vine to do. There is no command to produce fruit.

Life comes through the vine. What are we asked to do?

Part Two

Introduction to Part Two

Part two stories are summaries of my personal studies to understand these women who had to deal with difficult issues and challenging responsibilities, which are still issues and challenges for people in our time. The way each person dealt with their circumstances reflect cultural and political influences of their time and may seem controversial from our cultural perspectives.

Hagar's story occurred at about 1890 BC. She was of Egyptian heritage and became an employee in the household of a man called Abraham, who is the patriarch of both the Arabic nations and the Jewish nation. There was cultural conflict because Abraham's family were Mesopotamian, and their beliefs and cultural lifestyles were very different to the Egyptians. Hagar was an urban person working for a rural nomadic community. My study was triggered in a broader study looking at who the people were that God spoke directly to, recorded in the Bible. One of them was Hagar. Why is there so little written about her then? I hope you are inspired by Hagar as I have been and continue to be as one of the giants of great faith in the world's history.

Tamar lived about 1680 BC. She was a victim of domestic violence, dealing with violent behavior from a number of men in the same family. She seemed trapped and needed a very imaginative strategy to secure her safety. There is such a huge percentage of women (and a smaller percentage of men) who experience domestic violence. Everyone needs to understand how best to respond to domestic violence to address it when it occurs and prepare our children and grandchildren, so our family futures are safe.

Naomi had to leave her country because of famine in about 1270 BC and was a refugee settling in a neighboring country. After a number of years and personal loss, she returned to her home country. Naomi's story attempts to understand bitterness as a human experience and the importance of having someone who remains loyal through the long bitterness journey. Naomi's bitterness faded over time, and I hope her story gives hope to those whose life has brought bitterness to the soul.

Esther saved her nation from genocide in about 480 BC. The Jewish nation was living in exile at that time. Hers is a story of risk and courage. This is a study of the strategies and skills she used effectively in a highly charged political environment. I hope it is useful for those people living in risky environments and for those in leadership roles who are looking for important skills they should develop to be able to lead with integrity.

Deborah became the Judge of Israel in about 1250 BC. This study is my interpretation of her approach to leadership and that of Jael, who was a follower of hers. My intention in this study is to share those aspects of leadership that I admire and aspire to be in my own leadership roles.

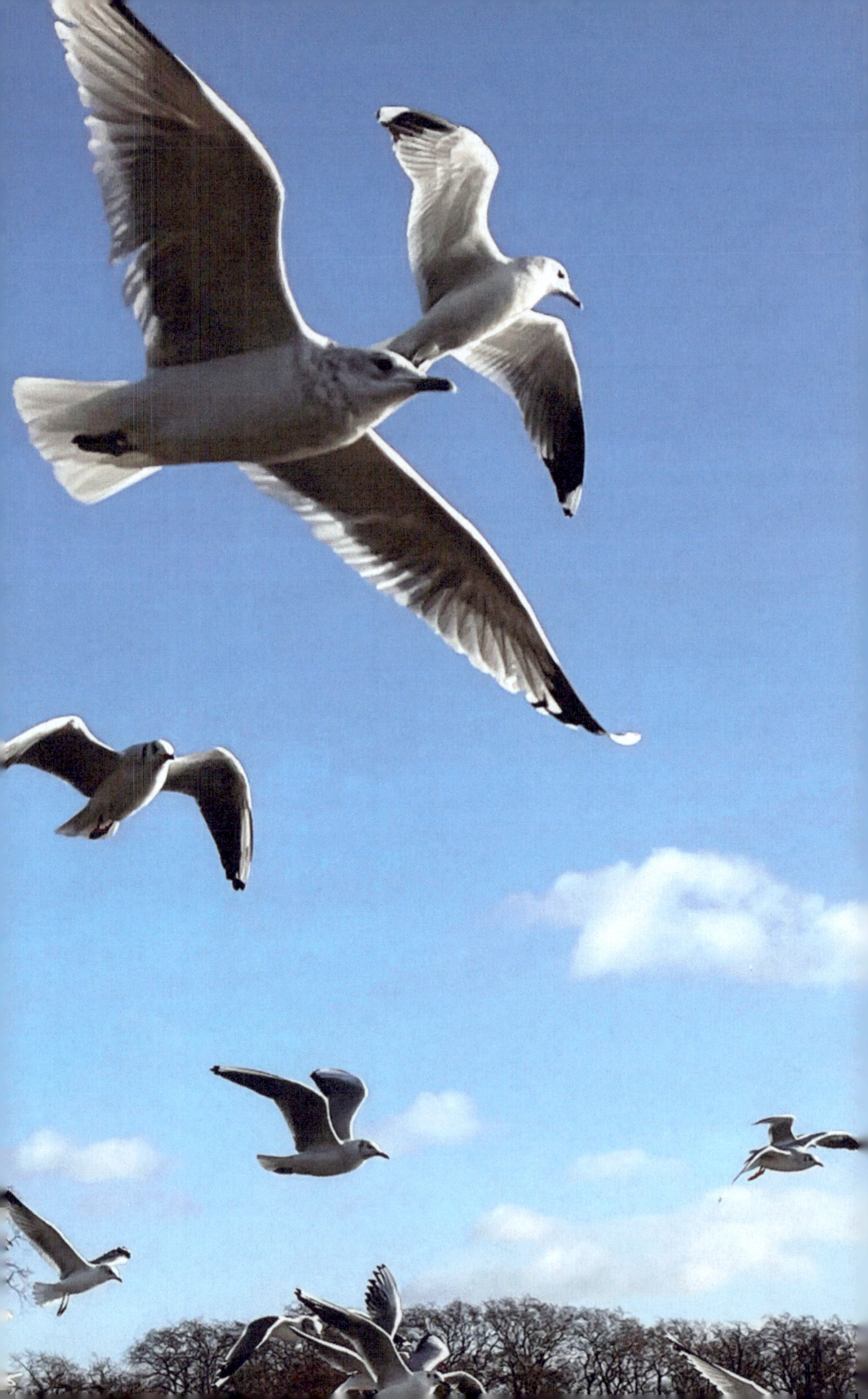

Hagar

1890s BC

Hagar's History

Hagar is the only person in the Hebrew Bible that gives God a name. She's one of the few people God spoke directly to in the Old Testament.

Hagar is not remembered well by Jewish, Christian, or Egyptian cultures. Producing an heir to Abraham brought her an unhappy relationship with Abraham, loneliness, and exile. The Koran does not tell the story of Hagar, though her story includes Mohammad's writings, the Hadith, where she is called Hajar, meaning "splendid" or "nourishing." She is honored in Islam faith as the matriarch of monotheism.

It's interesting to explore aspects of this ancient woman's experience.

What are cultural, personal, and economic costs to a woman in positions such as Hagar held?

What is the cost of a cultural ambition clash?

Were there regrets?

Were there memories she took pleasure in?

Were there times of wondering if it was worth it all?

How do we finish life well, and how do people who have had a contentious life at the end of life?

Her story starts with Abraham and Sarah.

Abraham was forty when he married Sarah, his stepsister. As newlyweds, they moved from Ur to Haran in Canaan because Abraham believed that God had made a promise to make from him a nation in this new country. They lived there for thirty years, but they didn't have any children. They made a move to Bethel, but it was dealing with famine so they went down to Egypt and set up business there for a year or so. They were important visitors to the land and became connected to the Pharoah. Arabic history confirms that while they were the guests of the Pharoah, they employed Hagar, an Egyptian woman from the area of Shur. Rabbinical commentators believe that Hagar was an Egyptian princess, given by Pharoah to Sarah. The job as Sarah's personal assistant would have had high status in the local Egyptian community so Hagar and her family would have felt very proud about this appointment.

When Abraham left Egypt, he was a very wealthy man, and he took all of his household back to Bethel. By this time, Abraham was in his seventies and Sarah was in her late forties, and they would have felt certain that Sarah could not conceive. As was the practice of childless couples in their local community, they adopted a son, Eliezer, to care for them. He was from Damascus and, at the time, God repeated His promise to Abraham that he would be the father of a nation (Genesis 12:1-3). Eliezer would have had expectations that he and his children would be heirs to Abraham's property and business.

Another decade passed, and then God renewed His promise to Abraham in a dream where God promised his son would be biologically his (Genesis 15:1-12), though there was no mention of Sarah. Sarah and Abraham lived in an area where there was a normal way to have a child that was biologically the father's child.

At that time, there was no understanding of an egg and sperm. People believed that the seed (sperm) was put into a receptacle; therefore, one woman was the same as another to produce an heir. In addition, the child, being only the product of a man, could still be raised by the wife and believed to be the mother. With their Mesopotamian heritage (coming from Ur), marriage contracts included the wife providing a concubine to produce an heir (Nuzi records). Also, Assyrian wives (their neighbor country) at that time could sell a slave concubine if she wanted to when an heir was born. Hammurabi code law is an ancient Babylonian ruler's code developed from Mesopotamian government and society laws, which demonstrated the contributions of Tigris Euphrates civilizations and used laws to reinforce class distinctions. The Hammurabi laws allowed wives to use a slave to produce an heir. After an heir was born, the slave could not be sold, but the wife could return her to being one of the slave women of the household.

So, Sarah gave Hagar to Abraham to produce an heir. Marriage was the acceptable Egyptian practice, especially for a person with high status, and it was common for Mesopotamian men to have multiple wives.

So, in this cultural context, Abraham married Hagar, his second wife, and also a secondary wife, and she became pregnant.

However, there was a huge cultural difference between the wives.

In keeping with Hagar's Egyptian culture, when a wife produced an heir, she could become the senior wife. Arabic history says that being pregnant made Hagar feel proud over Sarah, and Jewish records say that when Hagar knew she was pregnant, she felt contempt for Sarah, also saying that Sarah was harsh towards Hagar. What an unhappy house it must have been!

Sarah was not going to let an Egyptian culture displace her in the household, so she applied the Mesopotamian practice (later Hammurabi code) of Abraham's and her culture, and demoted Hagar to be one of the slave women—for Hagar, this was a demotion from being a wife of the boss and the personal maidservant of the wife.

Abram totally supported Sarah. He had no interest in Hagar, her culture, or her views, so Hagar fled into the desert. She realized that as far as Abram was concerned, he was unhappy in the marriage to her, and she left Abram's household and headed towards her previous home in Egypt.

There was no need for her to agree to live as a slave!
God sought her out. She knew He was God.
Amazing!
When God came to Abraham, he thought God was a traveler.
Joshua thought God was a man of war.
The men walking to Emmaus thought Jesus was a fellow traveler.
Christ will be to His followers what their faith expects and desires.
As with Joshua, God came to Hagar to encourage her to carry on with confidence, courage, and energy.

God found Hagar near a spring in the Kadesh desert (between Beersheba and Shur) and asked her to return, giving her the same promise He had given Abraham that same year. -God would multiply her seed exceedingly, and that her descendants would not be able to be numbered for the multitude (Genesis 16:10). He told her she would have a baby boy and that He wanted her to call the baby "Ishmael," which means "God hears" because God heard the distress Hagar experienced in her problems and struggle. He also said that Ishmael would be wild and have a lot of conflict between himself and other men, and that he would have control over all his family.

Hagar named the Lord "El Roi," meaning "You are the God who sees me," and she said, "I have now seen the One who sees me."

Genesis 16:13

Only one person has dared to give God a name—and she wasn't a priest or holy person. It wasn't Abraham or Jacob or Israel or David or Solomon. It wasn't any of Jesus's disciples.

It was Hagar.

She was humble, swallowing her fear and her pride, and returned to the household. She accepted being a slave in the house of her husband. From then on, Sarah (and Western history) referred to Hagar as the "bondwoman" or "slave woman."

When the baby was born, Hagar named him "Ishmael," and I am sure Abraham knew that God had spoken to Hagar and requested this name for their son.

Abraham and Sarah raised Ishmael as the biological heir of promise for thirteen years. Abraham did not have any information from God to think otherwise (as we sometimes experience in our decisions). We know that God didn't clarify the promise would be Sarah's son until Ishmael was a teenager (Genesis 17:16, 21) so it's a misplaced conclusion to say it was "wrong" of Abraham, Sarah, and Hagar to come to the decisions that they did. Ishmael would have known Sarah as his mother and that his father adored him. Hagar fed him as an infant, and he grew up knowing Hagar and that she gave birth to him.

When Abraham was ninety-nine years old and Sarah was in her early sixties, the covenant was again renewed. At this time, Abraham, Ishmael, and all the males of the household were circumcised to mark the promise. Visiting angels told Abraham and Sarah that Sarah would give birth to a boy. She laughed! At that time, they changed their names from Abram and Sarai to Abraham and Sarah and got on with making a baby.

For thirteen years, Abram had believed Ishmael to be his promised heir, and he loved him. So, when God told Abraham that he would have another son, he pleaded "if only" Ishmael could live with the blessing.

God replied that Isaac would be born to be the covenant nation, and He reaffirmed His promise to Abram and Hagar that He would also build a great nation through twelve children of Ishmael who would establish twelve tribes.

Just after the promise was clarified with Abram and Sarah, they witnessed the destruction of Sodom and Gomorrah so the household took off south to Gerar (near Shur where Hagar was from). Here, Abraham gave Sarah to the local king, Abimelech, saying she was his sister (they had the same father but different mothers).

What twists and turns for Hagar during that time! She was close to home; Sarah was given away to the local king to be his wife, and life was totally unpredictable. She stuck close to her son.

It wasn't long, though, before he had slept with Sarah, Abimelech found out Sarah was already Abraham's wife; he was a good man and returned Sarah to Abraham. Amazingly, Abraham, Sarah, and Abimelech parted as allies.

And then, at last, Sarah became pregnant, and baby Isaac was born.

When Sarah had her son, firstborn to her, she did not want to risk a challenge by Ishmael to land, inheritance, and covenant. She insisted that Hagar and Ishmael be removed from the household (just as Lot was moved out of Abraham's household to prevent an inheritance dispute many years earlier). Sarah saw Ishmael and her son together in the normal everyday activities of their family, and this "mocked" (threatened) Isaac's inheritance.

Sarah ensured that there would be only one heir–Ishmael had to lose his claim to family and to land. (This is one explanation for the reference to Isaac in Genesis 22:2 being the only son–that is, the only son with the covenant inheritance promised to Abraham.) Removing Ishmael from the household was a huge upset to Abraham because he loved Ishmael. Ishmael was now a young man; father and son had a strong bond, and he was growing up to be a fine young man that Abraham was immensely proud of. He would also have been distressed for legal reasons because local Nuzi law (confirmed in Nuzi tablets) prohibited the arbitrary expulsion of a servant girl's son.

Starting a Nation

When Hagar and Ishmael had to leave, Abraham provided food and water for them. She and Ishmael left the family in Canaan. They could not go north or east because that was where Lot and his family were established. They could not go to her homelands of Kadesh and Shur because of the covenant between Abimalech, Abraham, and Sarah. They had to go south to the desert of Peran. (In Islamic writings, Abraham took them to Peran, the desert area near Beersheba.)

They found themselves wandering in the desert around Beersheba and ran out of supplies. Hagar left Ishmael, who would have been fourteen or fifteen years old) under a tree, and went out of sight because she did not want to watch him die. Then she sat down herself and wept. An angel told Hagar that God was hearing Ishmael and not to fear. When she looked up, she saw a well and gave Ishmael a drink. The angel reminded Hagar of God's promise to her. He had promised that Ishmael's children would become a great nation and told her that God would be with Ishmael as he grew.

Hagar and Ishmael settled in the Desert of Peran (south of Beersheba and towards the Sinai Desert). Ishmael became an archer, and Hagar arranged a wife for Ishmael from Egypt. Hagar's male grandchildren, in order of their birth, were:

Nebaioth, Kedor, Adbeel, Mibsaan, Mishma, Dumah, Massa, Hadad, Temma, Jetur, Naphish, Kedemah.

Postscript

Arabic history tells of an ongoing relationship between Abraham and Ishmael and Ishmael's family. There is a record that Abraham visited Ishmael after the death of Hagar. This seems likely as when Abraham died at 175 years of age, his sons, Isaac and Ishmael, buried him in the place Abraham had bought and had buried Sarah when she died. You can read about it in Genesis 25:9,10.

The families of Ishmael settled in the area from Havilah to Shur near the border of Egypt as you go towards Assyria. Ishmael died when he was 137 years there in the area where the whole family lived.

Some years later, Esau, when he left Isaac's home after Jacob became the heir, went to Ishmael and married Mahalath, one of Ishmael's daughters, because he found out that his father, Isaac, had told Jacob not to marry a Canaanite woman. Mahalath was Esau's third wife, as he had previously married two Canaanite women against his parents' wishes.

Joseph's brothers sold him to a caravan of Ishmaelites and Midianites (second or third cousins, as Midianites came from Abraham's concubine Katurah, whom he married after Sarah died). Ishmaelites may have been business merchants working with the Midianites who traded for them. It is suggested that the Ishmaelites were investors who owned the goods and financed the caravans.

In the Islamic faith, it is believed that Abraham supported Hagar and Ishmael to begin the Islamic nations. Hagar is the "mother" as Abraham's wife and mother of his firstborn.

How do we know it was God who appeared to Hagar?

When angels appeared to people, they made clear that they were giving a message from God, and they did not let the person worship them. They sometimes reminded the person that only God is to be worshipped.

When God appeared, He was identified as "God" or as "the Angel of the Lord." On each occasion, He accepted the worship of the person or else the building of an altar to Him. He appeared (some say as the pre-incarnate Christ prior to being born to Mary) to

- Adam and Eve in the Garden of Eden
- Abraham, Hagar, Jacob, Moses, Joshua, Gideon, Samson's mother and father, and Samuel
- The crowd at Jesus's baptism by John the Baptist and Saul of Tarsus.

Walking Strong

Do you think of Hagar as the servant, Abraham and Sarah's mistake?

Do you think of her as Ishmael's mother?

She is an important person in the history of the world because she was the first woman God spoke directly to after Eve.

She dared to give God a name, and He respected the name she gave Him.

Hagar was an Egyptian woman who was employed as a senior member of staff in Abraham's household.

She married the boss.

She was his second wife, and Abraham married her to produce the heir who had been promised to him by God.

When she was pregnant with their first child, her husband didn't care how she was treated, and she ran away in fear.

Then she saw God, and He spoke to her.

While there was so much conflict in the household, to the extent that Hagar ran away, I am reminded of those verses in Matthew 5:

"Blessed are the pure in heart; for they shall see God.

Blessed are the humble, for they shall inherit the earth."

(Matthew 5:3,8)

These words describe how God saw Hagar.

The evidence is in the record but so often ignored.

She swallowed her fear and her pride and returned to the household to the lowest level job in the household, staying in it for about fourteen years.

That took courage and strength.

Her son was born and became his father's heir.

Abraham's first wife, Sarah, replaced Abraham's firstborn son with her new baby and the next year, at the request of his first wife, Abraham sent Hagar and her son Ishmael away for good. But God spoke to her again, and she found a purpose for living and had confidence to keep going because God believed in her and confirmed His promise to her.

Looking back, we know He kept His promise.

He was with Hagar and Ishmael during their lives, and she is the founding mother of the Arabic countries.

Hagar is a very important person in the history of the world, particularly for those who worship the God of Abraham.

Don't forget her.

There are not many records of God speaking directly to people.

She was the first woman God spoke to.

Whatever circumstances she was dealing with, Hagar held on to the "God who sees me."

That's walking strong.

Questions for Reflection

Hagar had great faith without anyone standing to support her.

How do you define faith?

Make a list of other people in the Bible who impressed God with their faith.

Whose faith impressed you? What do you notice about them?

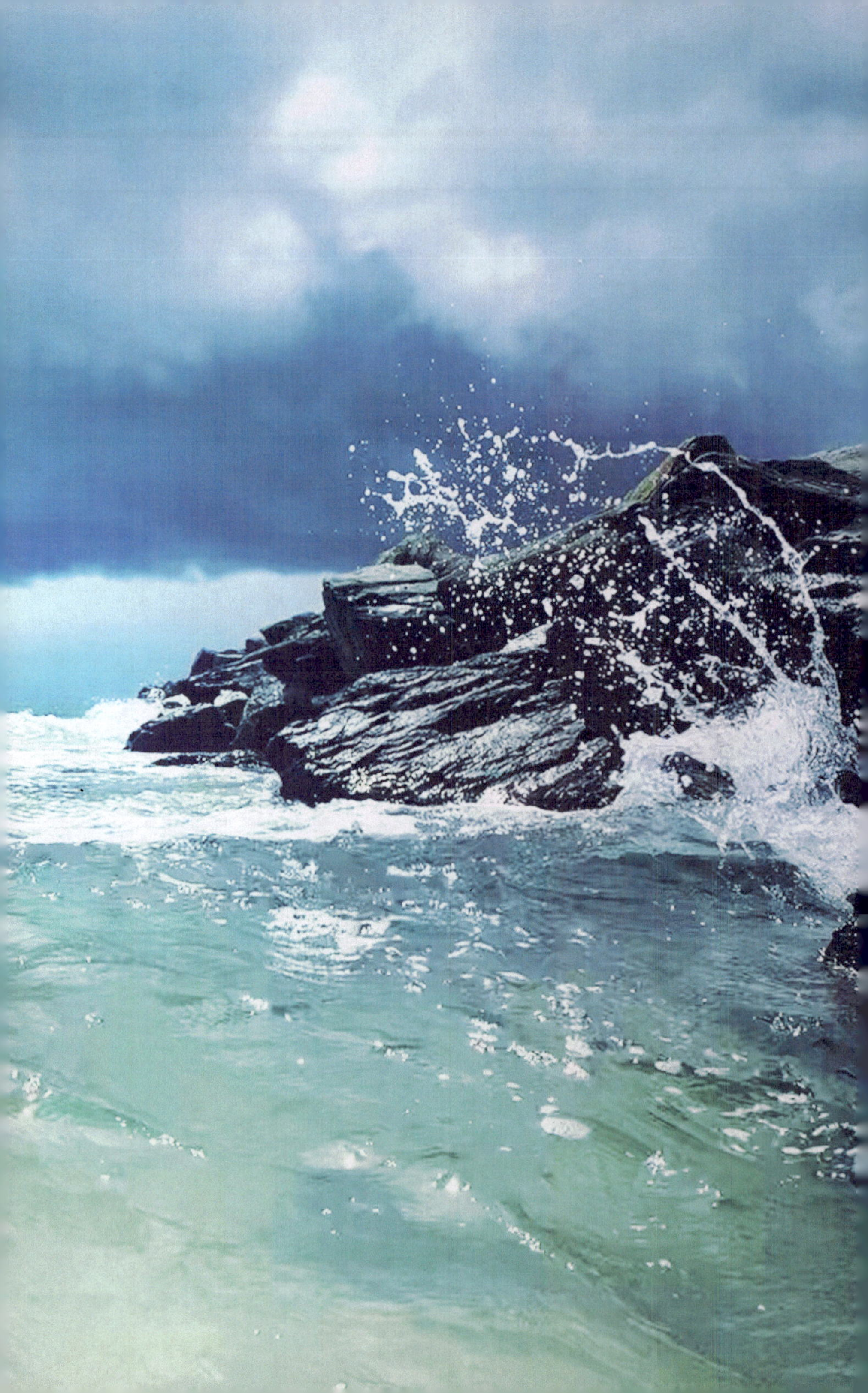

Tamar

Mid 1600s BC

This is the story of a community of men who didn't respect women.

Judah–Tamar's abuser

Judah's parents were Jacob and Leah.

Jacob, the son of Isaac and the grandson of Abraham, had two wives, two concubines (who started as his wives' maids) and twelve children. He was tricked into marrying Leah. He loved Rachel (Leah's sister) from the day he met her, and he'd negotiated with Rachel's father that after he had worked for Rachel's father for seven years, they could get married. When he lifted the bride's veil the morning after the wedding ceremony took place, he found it was Leah and not Rachel. He had it out with Rachel's father, and he married Rachel the next week. It wasn't a happy household as you can imagine. Jacob hated Leah.

Leah had the first baby in the family, and he was named Rueben. Her other sons were Simeon, Levi, Judah, Issaacher, and Zebulun. Rachel, however, was childless. In between Leah's children, Rachel and Leah were fighting because Jacob loved Rachel and hated Leah, so Rachel asked Jacob to sleep with her maid to produce children for herself. In retaliation, Leah insisted Jacob sleep with her maid as well to produce more children for her. Rachel's maid, Bilhah, had Dan and Naphtali to Jacob and Leah's maid, Zilpah, had Gad and Asher. After ten sons were born to the three women, Leah had the first and only daughter, who was called Dinah. And then, finally, Rachel became pregnant and had two sons called Joseph and Benjamin, but tragedy struck because Rachel died giving birth to Benjamin. These sons of Jacob from four wives formed the twelve tribes of the Jewish Nation and established the countries of Judah and Israel–now Israel.

Joseph became his father's favorite son, because he was Rachel's eldest boy.

Judah was the fourth son, but became the line through which Jesus was descended. Judah learned injustice from his father and conflict from the family, growing up being a tough, bitter, and aggressive person. He knew his father was a cheat. For example, he knew about the fear his father had of his uncle Esau (because Jacob had stolen his Esau's inheritance), and he knew the story about his mother, Leah, and had witnessed the conflict ever since between wives and also between his grandfather and his father. Judah knew how the two men cheated each other when his father moved their family away from his grandfather's household when Judah was four years old. Judah learned conflict within the family. For example, he lived with the conflict between his mother and her sister (his aunt) and the favoritism that his father showed his brother Joseph. (When he was afraid Esau would kill them all, he put Rachel and Joseph behind all of the other wives and children.) It continued when his aunt Rachel died having Benjamin. Judah had many observation lessons, and he learned his lessons well. He used his own behavior throughout the sons' growing-up years to become a leader within the pack of brothers.

The family settled in Canaan, and Judah's father bought land for them all from a Hittite man called Hamor. That meant Judah could set up his own property and started his family with a local Hittite girl called Shuah. They soon had three young boys. So, life continued between the community of local Hittites and the migrant Hebrew families. The families were growing, and the community prospered but it wasn't a happy place. Two significant events remind us that everyday life included conflict.

Firstly, the son of Hamor (his name was Shecham) raped Judah's sister, Dinah. She was the only sister of twelve brutal brothers, so what was Shecham thinking? And, yes, they responded in the most violent way they could imagine. Judah would have led the payback. They killed every male in the village and took all of the women, livestock, and wealth as "booty." One of the girls that Judah took was called Tamar. We'll return to Tamar's story.

Secondly, the brothers hated Joseph because he was their father's favorite with special privileges. Also, he was a "dreamer" (different to the pack), and he was an arrogant @#$%!!–he even told them about dreams he had where all his brothers bowed down to him. It was likely that their father would choose Joseph to be his heir, and they hated him for that. They talked about killing him and one day, when he came out to the site where the rest of the brothers were all working together, Judah said they should do it right there and then. The eldest boy, Reuben, didn't agree and convinced them to drop Joseph into a deep pit that was nearby. Reuben planned to help him get safely back to Jacob in secret and went off to put his plan in place. In the meantime, Judah saw traders passing by and decided to sell Joseph into slavery so they could make some money as well as get rid of the teenager. The brothers sold Joseph, split the money, and smeared his clothes with blood so that their father would believe that a wild animal had killed Joseph.

Getting rid of Joseph offered Judah his opportunity to become the son who would inherit the family property. He had three sons, and the eldest one's name was Er. To secure his position, he decided that Er needed to produce a boy that could be an heir, and he decided that he would give the child, Tamar, to Er to make that happen.

Tamar was abused.

Tamar was a little girl when her father and all the men in her family were murdered and she, with all of the women in her family, became slaves in Judah's household. They had lived through the terror of that massacre.

For Tamar, that day would have started like any other. She may have thought in the months and years that followed how strange it was that the day that change her life begin so ordinarily.

Another day that started just as the one before, but on this day, she was taken into Judah's household and forced to have sex with the man Er until she had his son. This young man had a reputation for being a thoroughly evil and violent person. In fact, he was so violent that he died young— soon after he took Tamar and left her childless and a widow.

But the abuse wasn't over.

Judah forced his second son, Onan, to try to make Tamar pregnant so that Judah would have an heir. Onan had other plans–his sons could be the heirs if Tamar didn't have children; so he had sex with her but made sure he withdrew before he ejaculated, and Tamar didn't get pregnant. Onan got found out and was killed–mysteriously, which freaked Judah out. In those days, women who had one husband die after another were thought to be witches, so he told her to get to her father's house and not to go near another man until his third son was old enough to get her pregnant. Living with ongoing violence, Tamar did as she was told. She was going back to hardship and starvation–the women in her family's house were prisoners of that household.

Judah was lying, too. He didn't intend to risk his last son getting killed if she was a witch. After a while, she worked that knowledge out.

*Domestic Violence**

For a full understanding of domestic violence and its pervasive nature, it is important to place the behavior in a social context. Violence is not a relational problem or issue; in reality, it is a social context giving men control over women. Domestic violence is a practice without recorded history because culturally, and in religious teaching, societies have given males superior status in relation to women. Violent men tend to act as if they have the right to be violent when they think it is normal, and also when they think it is justified. It is important to note that not all men are violent. As with other socialization processes, numerous influences in peoples' lives determine values and attitudes. Just as some men are more competitive and others are not at all competitive, some men have hierarchical, dominant, and violent attitudes, while others have more egalitarian, co-operative, and respectful attitudes towards women.

Myths about domestic violence include:

- alcohol causes violence.
- violence is more common in poor people's homes.
- violence is simply an extension of conflict or anger.
- violence is caused by stress.
- violence is provoked by women; they ask for it.
- violent men are psychiatrically ill.
- if a woman doesn't like it, she can leave.

Domestic violence can occur as physical abuse, sexual abuse, psychological abuse, social abuse, and economic abuse. Domestically violent people can be either the man or the woman; however, the cause and evidence demonstrate that this issue is almost entirely a male problem. Women find themselves trapped by a number of factors, including fear of reprisal, financial dependence, isolation, social stigma, emotional dependence, and poor self-esteem.

The victim, the abuser, or family and friends can stop domestic violence.

1. The Victim

Step One: Personal Safety. This means having a person to call, a place to go to, a means of getting there, and knowing what she will need to take at times when the cycle of violence begins.

Step Two: Understanding violence will not stop unless she takes action.

Step Three: Acknowledge domestic violence is not her fault and that she cannot live hoping the man stops being violent voluntarily—they rarely do.

Step Four: Get support to get through the processes to stop abuse. The support will include resources to make sure there is financial security, accommodation security, family security, and work security, as well as physical and emotional security.

Step Five: Link up with specialist services that provide individual support and/or groups of victims of domestic violence and groups for kids who have witnessed domestic violence in their homes.

2. The Abuser

Step One: Acknowledge violence is the issue.
Step Two: Get rid of minimization, blame, and denial.
Step Three: Talk about misconceptions about superiority in marriage and relationships.
Step Four: Obtain an agreement that he (or she) will stop the violence, seek counseling, join a group for the perpetrators of domestic violence, and be accountable for the situation.

3. Friends, Family, and Community Response

Addressing domestic violence must focus strong judgement on injustice and oppression. This will enable people to encourage victims of abuse to provide safety for themselves and their children, challenging abusers to take responsibility for their behavior.

*Adapted from "Domestic Violence It doesn't happen at our church...or does it?" authored by Valerie Cox, Eric Hudson and Greg Yee. Published in 1994 by Lifecare, an activity of Baptist Community Services, Sydney, NSW.

What did Tamar do?

It was about this time that famine affected the household, and Jacob sent his sons to Egypt for food supplies. During the trip, they came in contact with Joseph, who had become the national leader in charge of food supply. He had been the Pharoah's leader preparing for the famine and had control of all food supply during the famine. Although Joseph recognized his brothers, they didn't recognize Joseph, so he interrogated them, imprisoned the second eldest brother, Simeon, and insisted they return to Egypt with the youngest brother, Benjamin. On their way home, the brothers also found all of the money they had used to buy food supplies from Egypt had been put inside their sacks with the food.

When Jacob heard this, he would not part with Benjamin because he did not want to risk losing his only other child from Rachel (believing that Joseph was dead). All of them were afraid they would be killed on another trip to Egypt.

This was the time that Tamar acted to stop the violence.

Every day since the first day that Er forcibly took her and raped her, and then after his death the terrible thing that Onan did to humiliate her, she lived with memories and the knowledge that there was no husband and family future for her. Her heart would skip a beat, and she would feel the tears slide down her face. The memories would flow unbidden; a small thing would make her feel unsafe again, and she would feel the rivulets of sweat escaping from her hairline. She wanted to know why this man Judah did what he did to her, as her life was terribly altered by this abuse. Every decision she was going to make was coloured by wanting to feel safe.

It's different for everyone, but here's how she did it.

In the Hittite community, when a husband died, the wife marries the brother. If the brother dies, she is then to marry the father. It seems that this was the framework Tamar used to confront her abuser. Her focus was on safety and security for herself, and she found a way to confront Judah about his abuse.

At that time in Canaan, the ancient near-East tradition of prostitution and fertility cults were where local women who were devoted to the mother god (Ishtar or Anat) would reside at or near the shrines and dress in a veil as the symbolic bride of the gods Baal or El. Men would visit a shrine and use the services of the cult prostitutes on their way to planting fields, shearing wool, and during the period of lambing, which was the normal thing to do. In this way, it was supposed that they gave honor to the gods and re-enacted the divine marriage in an attempt to ensure fertility and prosperity for their fields and herds. (Walton, The NIV application Commentary Genesis, p669).

Judah's wife had recently died, and he was at the end of the mourning period. Tamar heard that Judah was going to a place called Timnath for the sheep shearing. (That is still the way of managing the flock—the shearers go to paddocks where the flock is held, and the major job of shearing is tackled in the shearing shed. The men work hard, eat big, play hard, and sleep sound.) So, Tamar set herself up at a shrine on the way to Timnath, and Judah visited the shrine. Judah saw her and thought she was a prostitute and said to her:

"Come now, let me have sex with you."

"And what will you pay to have sex with me?"

"I'll send you a young lamb from my flock."

"What will you give me to guarantee you'll send your payment?"
He said, "What will you take as a guarantee?"
"Your seal and its cord and the staff in your hand."
That was smart.
It guaranteed quick payment because a man used his seal all the time to conduct business.
They had sex, and then Judah went straight to the shearing and sent his friend back with the lamb to pay the prostitute. When his friend got to the part of the road where the prostitute had been set up, he couldn't find the shrine. He asked the men who were around.
"Where is the prostitute who set up here?"
They said "There haven't been any prostitutes around here."
So, he found Judah and told him. Judah was very frustrated.
"I sent the lamb to pay her, and she's taken off with my signature ring and my staff."
It would have been as frustrating as having your credit cards and toolbox or briefcase stolen.
Three months went by, and Tamar confirmed that she was pregnant.
She had what she wanted. If she could produce an heir to Judah, he became Jacob's heir as well. She knew she would be secure, and the abuse had to stop.
When Judah heard she was pregnant, he reacted immediately.
"Bring her here. She's been a whore. We'll burn her to death."
She was brought out of her home, and then she announced clearly to Judah's thugs who grabbed her:
"I am pregnant by the man who owns this seal and this staff. Do you recognize them?"
Judah was confronted, and he had to admit he'd had sex with her. Her strategy was not lost on him and he said:
"She's done this because she knows I need an heir."

Genesis 38:26

He didn't sleep with her again. I think he didn't go near her again, and she lived securely and without abuse.
She gave birth to twin boys, Perez and Zerah. That made her secure for life in that family.
The firstborn twin, Perez, became Judah's heir. Tamar could walk strong.

Postscript

By the time the brothers went back to Egypt, Judah was a spokesperson and leader in his household. He did all of the talking.

They had a difficult time from the Egyptian leader who kept finding problems with them.

When he knew the Egyptian leader had the upper hand over them, yet again with Benjamin, he tried no more tricks. He was brutally honest. This brought the Egyptian leader (who was Joseph) undone. He wept to see it. And then he told them who he really was–their brother—they were reconciled. I think that is an indication that Judah was learning to take responsibility and to develop co-operative and respectful behavior.

It was Judah who told his father Jacob that Joseph was alive. And when the whole household moved to Egypt so that Jacob could spend the rest of his life with Joseph, it was Judah who went ahead to meet Joseph and bring him to his father. Joseph threw his arms around his beloved father and wept for the lost years and the joy of being together at last.

Joseph settled all of the family in Egypt and gave them prime land and food rations according to the number of children they had. Judah's children who went to Egypt were Shelah, Perez, and Zerah.

Walking Strong

How many wives become hated by their husbands? Leah was hated by her husband from the day they were married.

I hope someone said to her:

"It's not your fault."

I hope she believed that.

What helped her to survive?

- She had the first baby in Jacob's family and the baby was a son–Reuben.
- She had the only daughter born to Jacob. Her name was Dinah.
- She was the mother of Jacob's heir, Judah, and grandmother to Judah's heir through Tamar, Perez.

In a funny way, Leah won in the end. She gave birth to the heir and is an ancestor of Jesus.

Everyone is valued by God. He looks at each person and loves them.

Every single person deserves equal respect and generosity.

Did she walk strong? I hope so.

When Jacob and his family moved to Egypt, Tamar held a strong position in the household because she was the mother of Judah's heir. She lived in her own quarters, had her own staff, and raised her own boys. She now lived in a land where women could hold very high status in families that were connected with the Pharaoh.

She was secure for life.

A few notes about women in Egypt:

Within a hundred years from Tamar's time, Egypt would have its first woman pharaoh named Pharaoh Hatshepsut, who reigned conjointly with her brother and then reigned alone after his death.

After that, Moses would be raised by one such woman, a daughter of the Pharaoh.

At the end of Joshua's life, Nefertiti was the powerful wife of the Pharoah Akhenaton, a couple who believed in one God and worshipped the god of the sun, Aton.

Cleopatra was the last Pharaoh, ruling in the last century BC (about sixty years before Jesus was born).

Tamar and Joseph had a lot in common—they had been victims of Judah's violence at the same time living in and through terrible experiences. They had found a way to rise out of and above abusive situations to positions of strength. They were able to acknowledge their shared experiences to each other when they met up again in Egypt.

Did Tamar share Jacob's family's strong belief in God?

They were such a dysfunctional family—hateful, fighting, cheating, selfish, bullying people. We all know people with faith in God like Judah and others of his family, and it's impossible to reconcile their natures with the God of the universe.

And then there was Joseph. He had their measure but he did not become like his father or his brothers. And in every circumstance, he had held firm to his faithful God, living his faith at work, with his friends and with all of those around him bringing salt and light into each day.

He and Tamar may have had those conversations as they remembered that terrible past. As with everyone else who came into Joseph's life, he would have encouraged Tamar and supported her because of their shared trauma. It's important for anyone who has lived through terrible times to have one person (or more) who is an encourager, someone who walks alongside you in the months and years to build a new future, someone who "lives" faith.

Someone who reminds us that we are valued and we can walk strong.

Questions for Reflection

If someone in your family or a friend discloses they are experiencing domestic violence, where are the services in your area that could provide support?

People experiencing domestic violence often feel like they are in a "fog," and it's hard to think clearly. They need practical help to start to build trust again. What can that look like?

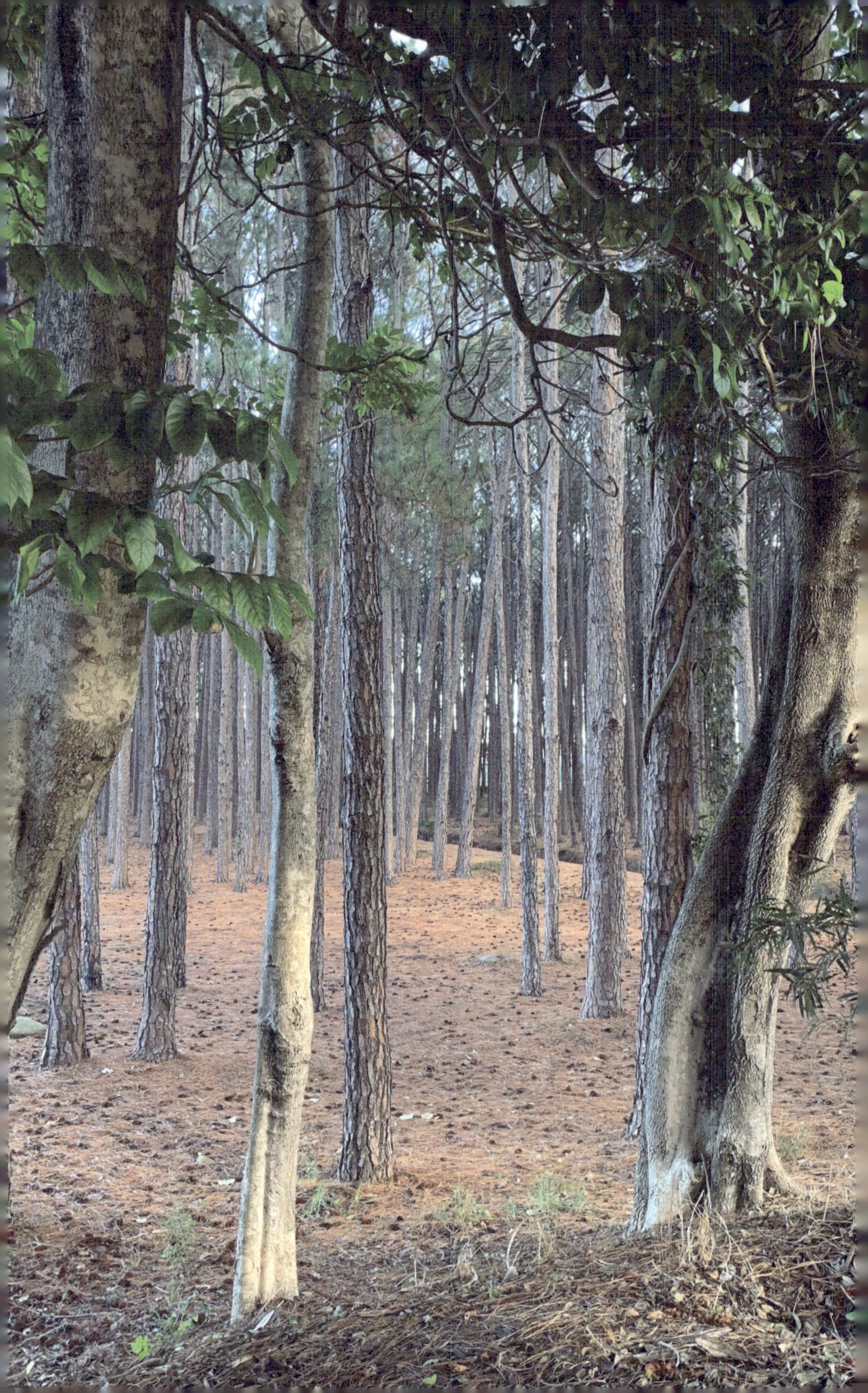

Naomi

Mid 1200s BC

Naomi lived in the part of Israel known as Judah, and in the time when Shamgar was Judge of the country. Israel's judges who followed Shamgar included Deborah, Baruk, Gideon, and Samson. At that time, the Israelites, having escaped being slaves in Egypt and being successful invaders, were now trying (and struggling) to adapt to a farming lifestyle and becoming a nation. Their neighbors were the traditional Canaanite communities whose main industry was agriculture, and who worshipped the god of agriculture (Baal) and his partner Ashterah.

Elimeleck and Naomi grew up in and lived in Bethlehem, but because of the famine, they decided to move to Moab to try and make a living. Bethlehem was a very fertile area and famine was rare, but the local civil unrest and skirmishes meant that in years when the usual crop production was disrupted, food was scarce for the community. Moab was a high plateau east of the Dead Sea, inhabited by Lot's descendants, so there were some distant connections. It was a big decision to move with their two sons because moving was costly and unsettling. They were also going to a community with a different religion and a different culture. They left their family behind and had to find a new place to live, new neighbors, new friends, new work. Once they arrived, there was no chance to change their minds and go back home.

So, they set to making a new life. Naomi developed good friendships with a group of local women–they were bringing their children up together. That made a huge difference when tragedy struck the family because Elimeleck died suddenly. Naomi had enough support to want to stay in Moab, and she continued the family business with help from the boys while she raised them. In time, both boys married lovely local girls–Mahlon married Ruth and Chilion married Orpah. These were very happy times for Naomi, watching the two couples establish their part of the home and plan their futures and build their dreams. Talking and laughter filled their home when they were all together, and her life felt full. The two girls were friends; she loved those girls, and they thought she was cool.

Before either of the couple had children, the two young men died–we don't know whether through sickness, injury, or war. What did Naomi think about death? She had lost her husband and her two sons before their time. The Jewish nation believed that to die was to "sleep with his fathers" and be "gathered to his people." Isaiah reflected the nations' belief that the Lord would "swallow up death forever" and that "the dead shall live, their bodies shall rise."

God allows terrible suffering in the world. Some think He might be all-powerful but not good enough to end evil and suffering, or else He might be all good but not powerful enough to end evil and suffering. The problems of tragedy, suffering, and injustice are problems for everyone. There are illustrations where evil events turn out for good. For every one of those, there is another story where there is no silver lining. The problem is based on a sense of fair play and justice. People, we believe, ought not to suffer, be excluded, die of hunger, or be oppressed.

The agony of the loss of someone loved, through death or when they tell you they never want to see you again, is a desperate feeling and may be profoundly mentally disturbing. When Jesus was facing the experience of His Father being cut off from Him, He found it unbearable. In the Garden of Gethsemane, the beginning of the experience put Jesus into a state of shock. As He was dying on the cross, He did not renounce God, but His cry had a ruthless authenticity. "My God, my God, why have you forsaken me!" It was a deeply relational cry, using words of intimacy as He was cut off.

Faith in God does not provide good reasons for the experience of pain, but it does provide deep resources for actually facing suffering with hope and courage rather than bitterness and despair.

Naomi didn't access these resources. She was bitter and decided to go back to Bethlehem.

Naomi and her daughters-in-law faced the problem of not having children and particularly an heir to continue the family name or claim the inheritance of the family. Naomi had some communication from Bethlehem and knew there was food again. There was going to be a good harvest in the coming months, and her family in Bethlehem sent news that the Lord was providing for them. Their faith in God stood firm.

She would have made her farewells to her good friends. They would have been curious about going back now and were sad to see her becoming bitter. They didn't want that.

"You are not a rosebud anymore, and you haven't taken a boyfriend or new husband here. You could hook an old millionaire in Bethlehem." One friend believed that bald men were sexy and intelligent.

Another friend disapproved of bald men. She argued that hair was a true symbol of sexual prowess–the local holy men shaved their heads to announce their celibacy. She spoke excitedly, "An unruly matted chest on a raised dome is simply oomph! That would turn me on."

"Why not find a young man? If I were single, I would try one," from another friend who was twice divorced.

"No moustaches for me. I like a clean-shaven man with big biceps," chuckled another.

"Too late to dream about that---you are married to an old man with few teeth and patterns of wrinkles all over his face and brown sagging muscles on his arms and legs, and you seem to prefer him," remarked another loftily.

"A woman like you may have a small mouth but can open it very wide."

In tough times, good friends bring smiles and laughter to a day.

It seems that Naomi intended to take her daughters-in-law back to Bethlehem. And so, they left and travelled for some time, but Naomi changed her mind and told them both to go back to their mothers' homes. She said to them, "Both of you go back to your mothers' homes. May the Lord deal kindly to you, as you have dealt to the dead and to me. The Lord provide for you a home, each of you in the house of her husband."

Ruth 1:9

Why did she change her mind?

She knew they were kind women (the word has the same depth as the word used to describe God's love, loyalty, faithfulness and covenant with Israel). Yet she believed or prayed that they would have no trouble finding new husbands by staying in Moab.

She also knew that in Israel, widows did not have the right of inheritance and were counted amongst the possessions of the family men. She was presenting a picture of hopelessness and despair at their circumstances because she felt it would be impossible to provide husbands for these foreign girls, so they could have children and heirs in her homeland. And she knew the laments of the prophets about unjust treatment of widows–it was a frequent theme.

The three of them were distraught. Naomi reminded them she was too old to have future sons for them. The two women were torn choosing between their love (loyalty and kindness) for Naomi and their hopes for a new marriage and motherhood. She must have been an exceptional mother-in-law!

In the end, Orpah went back home to her mother, but Ruth steadfastly continued on with Naomi to Bethlehem. When Orpah went home, her husband's

(Chilion) inheritance returned to Naomi. Naomi's grief, pain, and anger was deep enough for her to say to Ruth:

"It is exceedingly bitter to me."

She blamed God for the multiple tragedies that were hers to live with. There was no hiding of her feelings, no pretense that her anger was not there, no sweeping aside or "stiff upper lip," or false affirmation that all, in fact, will be well.

Naomi understood that capability of God to give good gifts (she affirmed to both girls her belief that "the Lord provide for you a husband"), and for His hand to be against you and that doesn't change your faith; it just changes the expression of faith. Her expression of faith in God at that time was a deep bitterness about God.

When they reached Bethlehem, she changed her name to "Mara," meaning bitter. She wanted everyone to know that she had had a full life, and now it was empty–that God had dealt very bitterly with her by bringing tragedy to her through the famine, the bereavement, the partings, a hopelessness in the foreseeable future, the loss of descendants, and family security. She acknowledged that God, Shaddai, the one who blesses can truly know the alternative story where meaningless and suffering are part and parcel of life each day. What does God feel about those people He has created who feel helpless?

When Ruth starting working and finding food to take home, Naomi was positive and encouraging. She was finding plenty of food. Naomi did not let her bitterness flavor how she supported Ruth. When she learned that the food Ruth was finding was from Boaz's farm, she explained the family connection. She and Ruth discussed their view that this family member was showing merciful and gracious lovingkindness towards Ruth, and that it was a sign of the hand of God in the circumstances of her life.

Naomi also recognized an opportunity. She told Ruth that Boaz was a close relative of Elimaleck's and encouraged her to stay close to the people around him.

She wanted to see what would happen.

She knew that, through their family customs and laws, that Boaz could take up Elimeleck's inheritance of land, and he could also father children that would be recognized as her son Mahlon's descendants. When Boaz encouraged Ruth to stay associated with his workers, Naomi decided to be an agent for Ruth and secure herself. She said to Ruth:

"I must see you settled in life" and gave her all of the instructions she needed so that Ruth could complete the local customs where a woman made her desire for marriage known to a man.

In response, Boaz acted as Naomi's agent with the closest kin to sort out if the closest kin were prepared to take over the land inheritance as well as Ruth. The closest kin could have taken over the inheritance of land, but he did not want to risk his own inheritance through new obligations with Ruth and Naomi. That is, he would have had to make a payment for the land and manage it, but the land would be the property of Ruth's child and not the child heir he already had. Boaz was free to marry Ruth.

This story has a happy ending.

The women of the neighborhood said, "A son has been born to Naomi." And they called him Obed.

Naomi was recognized as being provided with a descendant for her husband and son. Her place in the history line was secure.
Obed was the father of Jesse, who was the father of David who became the king of the nation.

Naomi took the son of Boaz and Ruth, whose name was Obed, and cuddled him to herself and became his nurse.

Walking Strong

Naomi had a lifelong relationship with God.

Through the support of her family and friends, she lived through the experience of bitterness and took opportunities to turn life around and let go of her bitterness.

She didn't see bitterness as sinful and understood it to be a reasonable reaction to the level of loss and tragedy she had to live with. In that bitterness, she continued to be totally supportive of her family (and they to her) and continued to live out her faith in the way she spoke about and maintained her relationship to God.

Questions for Reflection

Do you know anyone whose life is marked by bitterness? What does God feel about those people while they feel helpless?

There were times when David felt bitter, and he wrote poems that are included in the book of Psalms. Which are those, and what do they say about living with and through bitterness

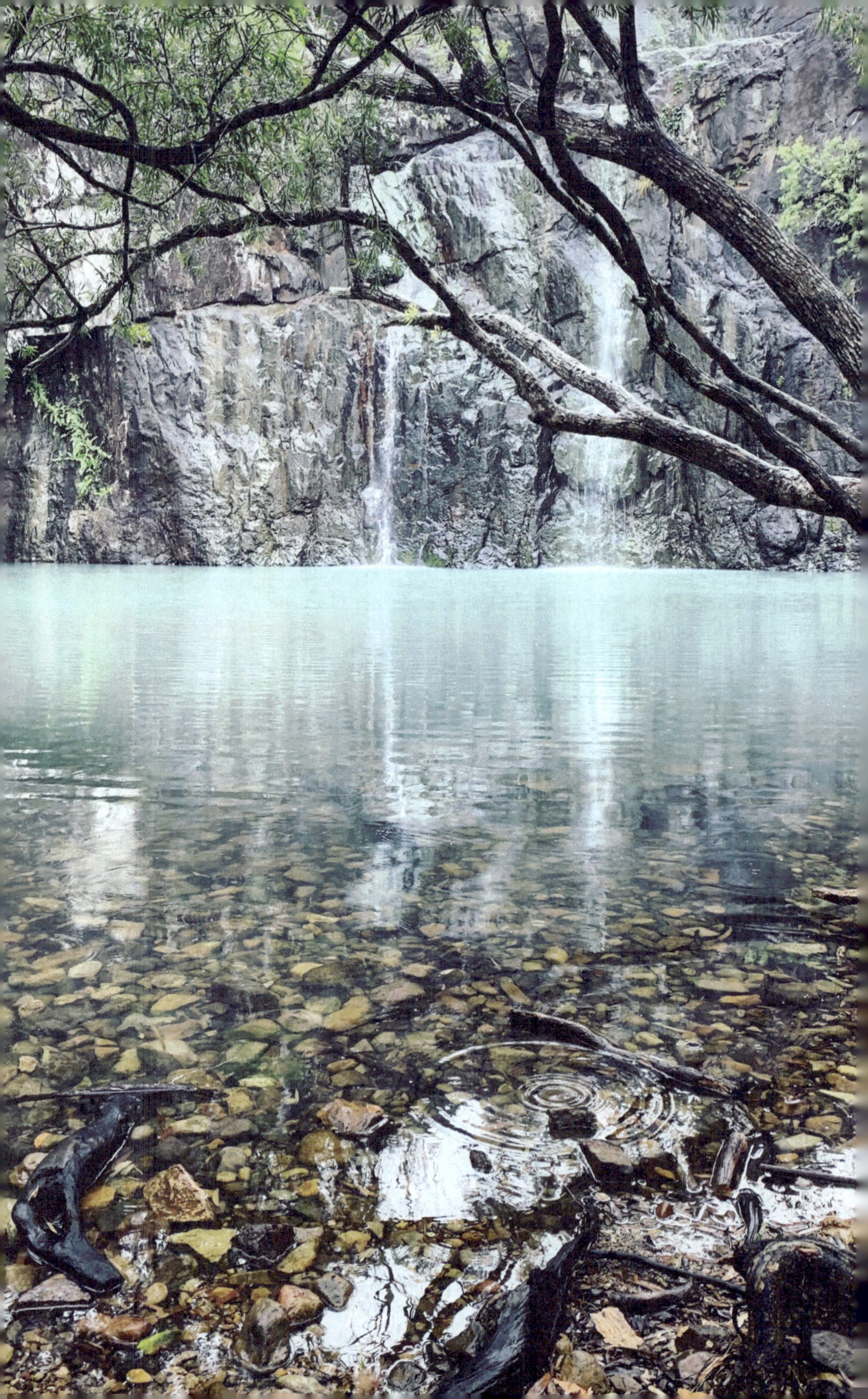

Esther

480s BC

Unlike most of the stories about women in ancient times, Esther is the central figure of the book called Esther. The book of Esther is written as a story, and you can read it as the seventeenth book of the Bible.

Esther lived in the time when the Israelite nation was in exile, though Ezra and Zechariah had started the restoration of the Israelite communities. Esther's rise was just prior to the time that Nehemiah started to reconstruct the city of Jerusalem.

Her story is a case study of leader decisions, political strategies, and ethical issues. Esther became a portrait of power and is remembered every year by her nation in the Festival of Purin. There are many books about leadership traits and leadership skills, yet there is not much written in Esther's story about either of these. She had a teachable spirit and followed through with her actions. They are a good start for a person who wanted to be a good leader. However, rather than retell the story or guess about her leadership skills, this is a study of the strategies she used effectively in leadership.

Decision Making and Ethics

Before Esther was a leader, she had a decision to make. She was a Jewish orphan being brought up by her older cousin in Persia, a foreign country. She decided to enter a contest where the king would pick a woman for himself to replace one of his wives known as Vashti. Josephus, the historian, believed that there were as many as 400 contestants in the beauty competition. The young women lived in the king's harem for a year and were given the resources to polish up their seductive arts, deportment skills, to pamper their bodies, and decide their cosmetics and wardrobe for the time they were each called to be considered by the king. Ultimately, it was a combination of elegance, charm, physical beauty, and erotic seduction that would carry the day.

Esther's decision to participate in the contest is controversial to this day:

As a Jewess, it was culturally important to marry a Jewish man and intermarriage outside her race was distasteful;

The contest required her to keep her nationality a secret;

To participate, she would have to leave the only family she knew and live shut up in a harem for the rest of her life;

It was a beauty and sex contest culminating in a night with a heathen king who might (only might) pursue a marriage which in every generation has a community moral and ethical issue to address;

Marriage would mean becoming one of many wives in the household of the king. Was it worth it?

Her second decision to approach the king and ask for Haman's decree (law and bylaws) to be changed came with extreme risks:

The king could order the death of any person approaching him without an authorization, including members of his household;

She was challenging a law made by the king's most senior advisor, which would result in large sums of money going into the king's treasury;

She had to reveal her identity, which she had now kept hidden from her husband, the king, for five years.

Everything is a decision. Everything is a choice. It comes down to that, the choices. How do we reconcile ourselves to the costs and rewards of the choices we make in our lives? We often don't even know if the choices we make are the right ones, and the jury is out until our children have children. Such was the case for Esther with her ethical dilemma.

Ethics is the decision-making process to determine whether what we plan to do is inherently wrong. In a society where everyone accepts a particular faith, that decision is based on what the Bible says, what the Koran says, what Buddha said, what the witchdoctor says, etc. In nations that have a multiple and/or no faith basis, ethics reflect and develop the concept of "secular sacred." This is an idea that some things deserve utmost respect and is explained by Margaret Sommerville in her book, The Ethical Canary as:

People must have profound respect for life, particularly human life.

People must act to protect the human spirit—the intangible, invisible, immeasurable reality to find meaning in life and make life worth living, a deeply intuitive sense of connectedness to the world and the universe; and

if something is not inherently wrong (that is, meets criteria a) or b)), people must also decide whether in all circumstances it is ethical to proceed and, if so, under what conditions.

If any of us were to explore this idea with a group of people in terms of Esther's ethical dilemmas, we would end up with a very complex summary. And from a modern perspective, women are ambivalent, feel discomfort, and disagree with using beauty and sex to gain opportunistic favors. And we know that what people say and what actually happens is not always the same. In some settings, women do use their physical appearance to gain advantage, and some men do not object or do not recognize that reality. A group is unlikely to end up with a shared view about the ethics of Esther's decision. She would have known that her predecessor, Vashti, had to manage the misuse of power in their male-dominated environment. Vashti's response to the problem she faced was an emphatic "No," and she is a model to many women and men alike who take their stand against human indignity.

Imagine the many discussions, debates, and plans her uncle and guardian Mordecai and Esther had before they settled to their choice and embarked on this risky strategy.

However, having made the decision to participate (with the support of Mordecai), Esther needed to be strategic in every future decision and action. Esther, who followed Vashti into the same context, chose to work within the structures of the system to achieve her goal.

In an ongoing climate of tricky politics, the strategies Esther and Mordecai used and responded to included:

Influencing and Alliances

Esther's primary ally was her cousin Modecai. He held a position in the Persian Court and together, they made and delivered a smart plan. Together, they put actions into place to maintain their positions and become powerful. These plans included:

Entering Esther into the beauty contest to be influential within the harem, and perhaps as the winner of the competition. With either result, Esther was in a position with some access to the king's family and staff.

Concealing Esther's identity.

Esther means "star," and she was also known by the Jewish name Haddassah. There is some commentary that neither of these names may have been the name she used in day-to-day life. This strategy was another ethical dilemma. In Daniel's case in Babylon, it was important for him to be known as a Jewish man who lived out his faith in God. Esther, on the other hand, kept her identity hidden at the Persian Court until the critical moment when she used it in a strategy to save the Jewish people living in Persia.

Once Esther was in the harem, Mordecai met with her daily. This was an important part of communication strategy to keep Esther linked with her community, for the two of them to be able to strategize, to identify risks and opportunities and manage those, and solve problems together. Mordecai would also have been there to teach Esther a lot about the court–how it worked, the people dynamics, the politics of the court, the developing laws of the country. This would mean that Esther would have interests in common with the king, and their conversations would have been lively, spirited, and energizing.

Mordecai located himself in a house near the court gates. He was in a strong position to know all that was going on as soon as it happened.

When Haman had died, Esther negotiated for Mordecai to be appointed to Haman's old position as the chief advisor to the king.

Hegai was the second critical ally. He was the eunuch in charge of the beauty contestants. She immediately built a good supportive relationship with him so that she gained his full support. The literal translation was that "she lifted up grace before his face." That would have contrasted to the rivalries, in-fighting, and envy in the harem. Seeing her potential, he assigned seven maids to her for the year's preparations. Perhaps some of them had prepared or waited on other wives and concubines for Xerxes. They would have had valuable advice for Esther. Hegai gave her advice too, particularly when it came to be Esther's turn to spend the evening and night with the king, and Esther requested from the king the things that Hegai recommended. He also gave her very good quarters inside the harem and organized her preparation–beauty treatments, deportment lessons, food, education, and contact with appropriate palace networks and friends of the king.

Xerxes (also known as Ahasuerus) was the main strategic alliance sought by Esther and Mordecai. He had removed Vashti (his queen) in the third year of his reign and then gone immediately to war with Greece. The historian Heroditis considered Xerxes to be one of the three most formidable Persian kings (the others were Darius, his father, and Artaxerxis, his son), but Xerxes lost the war with Greece after four years and returned to Persia. Heroditis described him as tall, handsome, ambitious, ruthless, a brilliant warrior, and a jealous lover. Following the war with Greece, Xerxes held the beauty contest to find a new wife and when he called Esther, she immediately won his affections. Five years later, when she had to confront Haman's actions with the king, she had to secure his alliance elegantly, as she was not confident of the king's attitude towards her. She may have been afraid, but that did not drive her tactics of laying a strategic groundwork to ensure a successful appeal.

She had to be sure that even though the king was willing to grant her a request, they had to spend some time together on a number of occasions, where she included Haman, to re-establish the king's confidence in her knowledge and expertise. Having committed to honor her request at each dinner, the king was more committed. This was very important, because it was her life that she was going to ask for. She was even more successful because she made that request with Haman present, and he was caught completely off guard. Once her request was granted, in front of her enemy, she requested that it be extended to all of her community. He, again, stood by her as her ally.

Congeniality and Discernment

Esther modeled grace before the people in the king's court. The skills of grace-filled charm and elegance she brought with her to the harem, and it meant that she found favor with the influential head eunuch, Hegai. Part of her strategy when she entered this competition was to get on with people. It made her a standout.

And she maintained this approach throughout her story. Esther showed clear direction to reach her goals, restraint and control, modesty, loyalty, and authenticity throughout this book.

These are traits of leaders who find that others want to follow them.

Discernment to recognize the good or bad in what another says.

She heard the advice of Mordecai and Hagai and acted on their advice because she had confidence that they would give good direction to her.

She would have used the discussions with Haman and the king during their two banquets together to contrast herself with that of Haman. Haman may have talked about the upcoming lawbreakers who were going to be executed! She let enough conversation go by to ensure that the king discerned the arrogance and heinousness of Haman and her integrity and honesty when she described his atrocity.

Adapting to Changing Circumstances

The story of Esther is one of a young girl who used aliases and was living a compliant, passive life in a foreign country. She transformed, using her beauty and developing strategic skills, from being an unknown to become a powerful leader and a national heroine.

Esther used prudence, chance, and fortune to adapt to changing circumstances—Vashti had been removed after publicly refusing an order from her husband, he had lost a war after four years of resources and effort–and Esther took the opportunity to gain a place in the King's circle. This was an enormous risk to take and presented a number of problems to confront. Even though she would be living amidst great wealth and status, after one night with the king, these women lived the rest of their lives in the harem. They could not leave to marry or return to their family. They would not see the king again unless he asked for them by name. Children conceived by the king to any of these women were raised to serve the king in high positions but could not become legitimate heirs to the throne.

Once she was in the circle, she continued to be well-regarded. A few years down the track, she did not waste any time in using a range of strategies when she was required to protect her nation, which included the usual protocols and practices of a woman in her position towards the king (with the exception of approaching him once without an invitation). She acted in a way to gain high favor with the king, and her requests were more likely to be considered.

Religion

Religious political strategies colour world history in all nations and all cultures –between Catholics and Protestants, between Christians and Moslems, between religion and atheism–no culture has been immune. The core agenda of this story is Haman's strategy to instigate the genocide of the Jewish people living in Persia.

Throughout history, minority groups have suffered this atrocity. Haman's agenda was a personal retaliation because he had expected the people of the court to bow to him, and Mordecai refused. Haman plotted to kill him on the pretext that it was because he was a Jew. The way he built his strategy was through a discussion with the king that there was a minority group who were acting unlawfully, and that they should be killed on a specified date. In return for implementing this act, the king would receive a significant revenue increase into treasury.

When Mordecai heard of this retaliation, he went into public mourning. He did not go near Esther and was beside himself with grief.

In the end, it was up to Esther to use a range of subtle strategies to respond to the heinous strategy of this powerful figure in the king's court.

Gaining Honors and Heroism

Shortly after Esther became the king's wife, Mordecai uncovered a plot to kill the king as he was, by then, living close by. Two of the palace officers who were guards at the gates of the palace, Bigthana and Teresh, were angry with the king and planned his assassination. But they were overheard, and Mordecai came to hear about it so he told Esther who passed what Mordecai had heard to the king.

This strategy lifted the profiles of both of them to the king.

When the king's investigation confirmed the plot, the two men were hanged. Mordecai's support for the king through this action was recorded in the king's annual report.

Sometimes comic twists happen!

At the time when Haman was putting his plan to kill Mordecai in place, the king had a sleepless night! So, he had his annual reports read to him (that would put many people to sleep). He realized he had not honored Mordecai for uncovering the plot and as morning came, and Haman came in to work, the king said to him;

"What should be done for the man the king delights to honor?"

Haman recommended a reward that he would like—only to see it given to his challenger and enemy, Mordecai.

When was it that Esther realized she was going to be a heroine?

Mordecai sent the message through one of her trusted staff–telling her the situation and asking her to go to the king to beg for mercy and plead with him not to have the Jewish people killed. Her response was:

"All the kings officials and the people in his provinces know that for any man or woman to approach the king in the inner court without being summoned, there is one law: that he be put to death. The only exception to this is when the king extends his gold scepter to the person and spares his life. But it is thirty days since I was called to go to the king."

Mordecai sent back a pressured response. He was strategic.

Now's the time! You are in the right place to change things!

So, speak up! Don't be silent!

He said, "Do not think that because you are in the king's house you alone of all the Jews will escape. For if you remain silent at this time, relief and deliverance for the Jews will arise from another place but you and your father's family will perish. And who knows but that you have come to a royal position for such a time as this."

Esther 4:12

She then knew there was another plan that would exclude her and her family. So, she wanted them all to know her risk–whether it became a success or failure.

Esther accepted the challenge.
This was the turning point.
Her words reveal enormous faith combined with courage:
"Gather together all of the Jews in Susa and fast for three days. My maids and I will do the same.
Then I will go to the king even though it's against the law.
And if I perish, I perish."
Esther, at that time, had to plan the strategy alone. It was no longer safe for Mordecai to work on it alongside her. She had to courageously face the king and then find a way to unmask Haman.
She did it. She became a heroine to that Jewish community who fasted for her and did it in a way that she strengthened and intensified her power in the royal court.
In preventing the annihilation of Jews at that time in Persia, she is remembered still as a heroine.

Discrediting

Stewardship of power is a major theme for leaders. This story exposes what happened under the pretense of law and justice by the man Haman. History is marked by others like Haman who have risen to power only to have their flaws exposed.

Esther negotiated for the king and Haman to attend first one banquet, and then a second banquet. Once she was satisfied that her alliance with the king was secure during their second banquet together, and while Haman was present, she started the delicate and dangerous task of accusing Haman while not incriminating the king (who had approved the massacre). She had to incite the king against his friend and advisor without bringing the king's anger towards herself. She used all of her strategic skills and spoke obliquely, making sure she used Haman's exact words—though she delayed saying Haman's name.

The king had just said to her for the third time,
"Tell me what you wanted to ask me for. I'll say yes to whatever you ask. Now tell me what's on your mind and what you would really like."
She said,
"If I have found favor with you, O King, and if it pleases your majesty, grant me my life–this is my petition. And spare my people–this is my request. For I and my people have been sold for destruction, slaughter, and annihilation. If we had been merely sold as male and female slaves, I would have kept quiet, because

no such distress would justify disturbing you."

The king said, "Where is he? Where is the man who would dare to do that [to you]?"

Esther replied, "The adversary and enemy is this vile Haman."

The king was in a rage! His honor was offended that Haman had attempted to harm his queen and her community. He left the dinner table and went to the garden.

Haman was terrified and started pleading with her. He was so distraught he fell on her, just as the king walked back into the room.

He roared out, "Will he even molest the queen while she is with me in the house?"

The man was totally discredited.

Military Protection and Action

Esther requested that the Jewish people fast for three days before she went to see the king and plead for mercy against the genocide. In that strategic action, she took the leadership of that group of people and responsibility for their future. They were willing followers.

After her success, she cemented her leadership with follow-up actions that reflect the usual practices of their history. She ensures the deaths of Haman's sons, then that the bodies be impaled for public humiliation. Finally, she and Mordecai reversed Haman's decree and legalized killing of those who were the Jewish people's enemies throughout the empire. Esther went further and extended the time permitted for killing their enemies.

This is a difficult and troubling strategy. The issue of the treatment of enemies is a reminder that both men and women may support killing. The ethics of the story as it unfolds is disturbing in any attempt to justify the slaughter at the end of the story. In her book, Katherine Sakenfield reminds us that in our own time, we have to acknowledge it is difficult to distinguish between preemptive defensive strikes and uncalled-for aggression, between actions based in revenge and those based in legitimate fear for personal and communal safety (2003, Sakenfield K. D., Just wives? published by Westminster John Knox Press, Louisville, Kentucky).

The people were delivered, and it was an early example where God's people did not experience miraculous deliverance, but the normal outworking of the ethical and political flaws within society.

Perhaps there is reason to consider God's strategic use of the event.

In the NIV commentary on the book of Esther, Karen Jobes writes:
Saba explains that this great deliverance achieved without miracles was the reason the Jewish people finally came to rest their faith on the Torah, the Word of God, rather than miraculous displays of his power. The story of Esther implies that what God's word decrees will happen, even without miracles. God's omnipotence is truly great. (1999, Jobes, K. H., Esther; The NIV Application Commentary, published by Zondervan, Grand rapids, Michigan).

Walking strong when God is invisible

The book of Esther is the only book of the Bible that does not mention God anywhere in its pages. God is invisible.

When we think of redemptive history, we think of the great miracles and the displays of God's power. But the history of the Jewish nation and the Christian redemptive story is linked together through seemingly insignificant and ordinary decades and centuries. People through those times, and people today, make decisions unwittingly that have long-reaching consequences far beyond what they could, and can, foresee. In all of these times, God moves history forward to accomplish His ultimate plan to the time when Jesus returns, and eternity begins for all of us.

Many people in their work life and their community life, including church communities, face political strategies. As in Esther's time, this brings confronting challenges and problems, particularly as the best-known political strategy writer in early years was Machiavelli, whose book titled Prince became known for favoring expediency over morality. To be "Machiavellian" is to be offensive, obnoxious.

The story of Esther gives leaders confidence that they can develop strategic leadership skills to:

- Work honestly and with integrity,
- Build trust and respect,
- Lead with clarity, engagement, and accountability, and
- Enable others to learn and develop their strengths.

This is a model of servant leadership. As leaders promoting justice, mercy, and peace, we know that tactics (strategies) matter, and we need not get caught up in fighting about the best way to challenge and change the power patterns on the world (or the place in which we work and live). Over the time it takes for change to happen, a variety of approaches (strategies) will be needed.

Some think it is easy to look at other people's decisions and know clearly what is right and wrong. Some believe that God will give the wisdom to know what to do and the moral strength to do it. For some, talking about ethical and moral issues is abstract, theoretical, and it is possible to describe the situation in simple dot points, making choices clear. But life isn't neat and tidy. There comes a time for all of us when we find ourselves in a situation that is not clearly defined, and every choice is a troubling mixture of good and bad. We pray, believing God will give us the wisdom and strength to find and do the best thing. We search the Bible with open hearts in situations that biblical teaching does not directly address. While we are doing this, situations move on by default or deliberate action, and we make decisions, ready or not. And in those times of great struggle, the last thing we need is for others to make simplistic and moral judgments.

Esther's story gives us encouragement and comfort when we face an odd mix of ethical issues. We can be responsible to God for living faithfully in every situation as best as we know how. Even when we make poor decisions, God is able to perfect His purposes in us and through us. Charles Swindoll, in his book titled Esther, wrote about Habakkuk, who watched unjust events occur over and over and finally, he could take God's silence no longer and cried out, "Why? And while I'm at it, how long?"

Life is filled with sustained periods of silence. Often the turning points of life, the significant events, are subtle.

Esther may have looked back with regret or shame, or she may have looked back with a clear conscience, knowing she acted as best she could at each step. In either case, her history shows that she could leave the decisions with God and move on walking strong.

Questions for Reflection

For some, there is a sense of God during difficult circumstances.

For others, God seems absent.

How do we best support someone who says, "I don't have any sense of God now" or "I'm not hearing anything from God."

Esther was young (perhaps still a teenager) when she was asked to do something that could cause her to be killed for doing it.

What are things that you would be prepared to die for?

Have you ever paid a price to "stand" for something? Would you do it again?

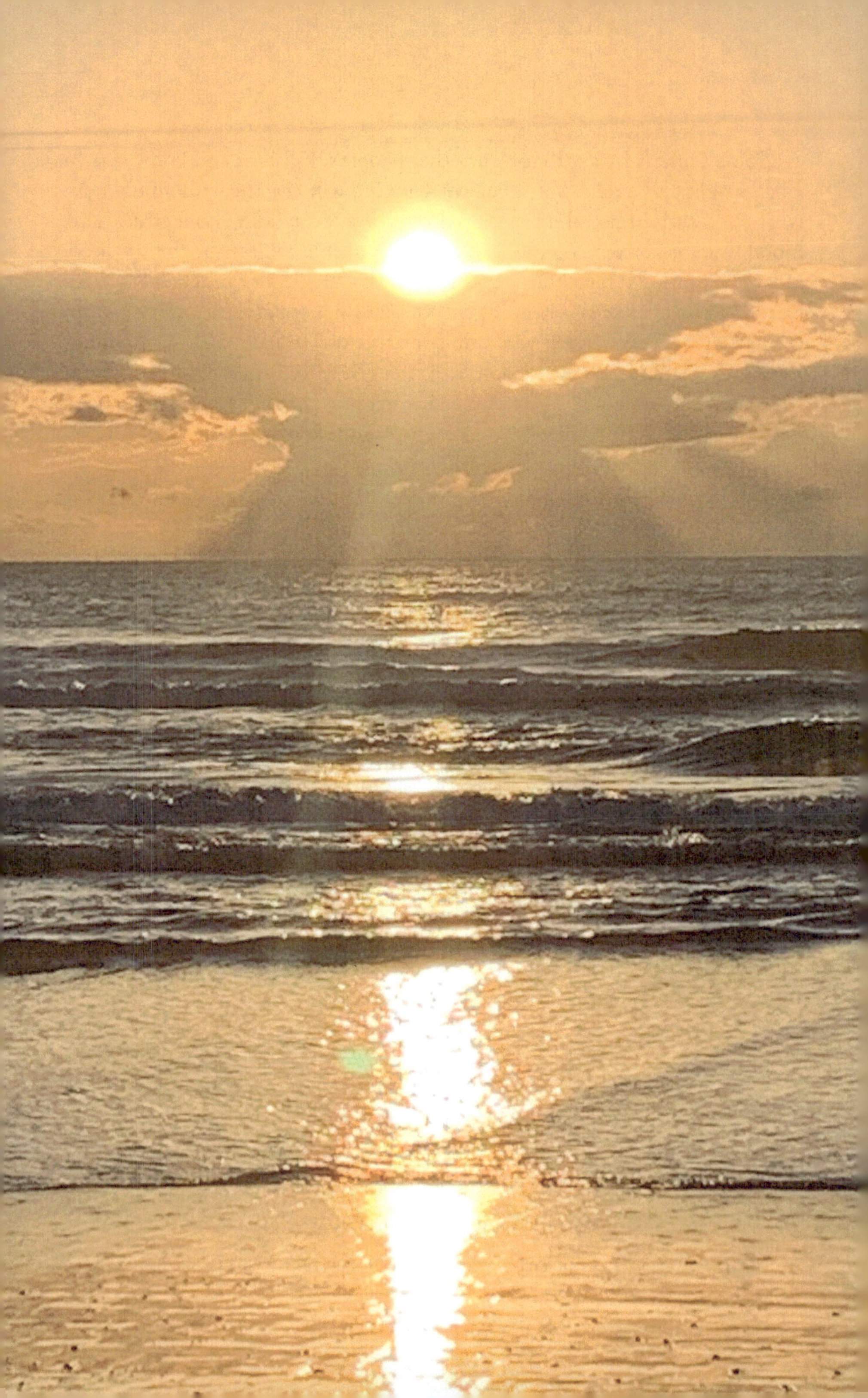

Deborah

1250s BC

The Israelite nation had settled in Canaan. After Joshua, Israel appointed Othneil as judge; he was Caleb's nephew. While fighting between Canaan and Israel was frequent as the new nation settled in the area, Othneil and Ehud were able to establish long-term peaceful relationships with the neighboring Canaanites.

Then followed Judge Shamgar, who was not able to establish peace between the Israel and Canaan. Canaanite mercenaries, led by Sisera, used Canaanite's army iron chariots to oppress the minority communities for over twenty years. His 900 chariots were used as a killing platform to regularly and mercilessly pursue and slaughter minority groups in the area.

The Israelite people abandoned any public roads and places. They used the back roads and stayed out of sight, living life hiding and hungry. Atrocities were whispered in the night, and days were spent in quiet fear.

During those years of genocide, a woman called Deborah had a calling on her heart. She had watched the slaughters, the bashings and theft of young girls to be mercenary slaves. In this environment, she set up her business under a tree, a palm tree between Ramah and Bethel. She spoke with divine authority, empathy, kindness, generosity, and compassion.

Her personal warmth was balanced by steeliness.

Deborah was courageous and decisive, experienced in settling disputes that were intractable and unable to be resolved by local arbiters.

She became a national leader as the Israelites were crying out against the outrageous cruelties their people were suffering.

Deborah acted quickly and without hesitation. During the period, she moved from being a sage whose advice people sought and respected to being the national leader and judge. She may have, just a few hours after one attack, addressed these mercenaries directly, saying something like, "You may have chosen us today for your games, but we utterly condemn and reject you."

She may have called to others:

"I implore you: speak the names of those you have lost, rather than the name of the man who took them. The mercenary may have sought notoriety, but we in Israel will give him nothing. Not even his name."

The communities grew a focus for their energy—remembering the names of the victims. Deborah galvanised the community and offered a clear and strong call to action.

Deborah became the first female national leader of the Jewish nation, the fourth judge of Israel, taking over from Shamgar. Her headquarters remained between Bethel and Ramah, near her home at Ephraim. She was a descendant of Ephraim and the wife of Lapidoth.

She established her position with wise, strong leadership, being very focused on looking after the people who are most affected straight away. The rabbinic tradition described her leadership style as fair, open, and refusing to show partiality. She favoured a team approach—willingly recognising those who worked with her and encouraging them to develop as leaders.

She had a God-given gift of prophesy and through this gifting had huge influence. Holding true to the God of Israel, she inspired people to hold hope over fear in a very practical conversation about solutions to the problems.

In this context, she called a meeting with Barak, the commander in chief of the Israelite army. The locals described these soldiers as "warriors who had become fat and sloppy—men who had no fight in them."

She took with her the captains from Ephraim, Benjamin, Makir, Zebulun, and Issachar. She told Barak that with this group, Naphtali would join them, and God had given her a prophetic hope that they would defeat their oppressor. Her plan was this:

- Barak was to take ten companies of soldiers from Naphtali and Zebulun and meet her at Mount Tabor to prepare for battle.
- Deborah would, with the other captains, draw Sisera to the Kishon River with his troops and chariots. That way, Barak could attack and win the battle.

It was a good plan. Barak would have safety from the iron chariots as they met in the uneven and wilder area of the base of the mountain, as Deborah drew them along the river plains into a trap. Then it would be a man-to-man battle, sword on sword, spear on spear, with the chariots unable to mow Barak's soldiers under.

Barak did not agree.

Barak told her, "If you will go with me, I will go. If you won't go with me, I won't go." Barak wanted the influence of Deborah in keeping with local Assyrian pattern of having a woman prophetess to inspire the troops and taunt the enemy. The Assyrians, too, had women warriors. The people who were there at the time probably found nothing strange in Barak's request.

It didn't sit well with Deborah, who had provided him with a prophetic plan.

She was a new leader, and she needed Barak to recognise her leadership. She needed this first follower to get this battle going.

Having a great first follower would make all difference between standing alone, getting full buy in and acceptance from the nation she was leading. She had the right person, but the wrong attitude in her first follower.

I think she had to have great trust and hope that she had God's leading to go forward in the way that she did.

Deborah warned him in prophesy.

"Of course I'll go with you. But understand, with an attitude like that, there'll be no glory for you. God will use the hand of a woman to take care of Sisera."

Judges 4:9

And so, she went with him to Mount Tabor. There they prepared for battle on the mountainside, protected.

Meanwhile, Sisera heard about Barak's activity through his military intelligence, one person in particular, a man called Heber. Heber was a distant relative of the Israelites through Moses but had severed his ties. Sisera called his troops together, and they travelled up, choosing to go the quickest route along the Kishon River flats.

Deborah and Barak watched as they raced up towards Mount Tabor, and Deborah said to Barak, "Has not the Lord gone ahead of you? Go!!"

And then the strangest thing happened.

Further upriver, heavy rains had been causing the river to rise for days. As the army raced towards the Israelites, there was a breach along the riverbank, causing the side to collapse into the swollen river and tons of water rushed across, flooding the Kishon river plains.

Sisera saw the wave of water coming and fled on foot away from the battlefield and back to Heber's house.

The waters swirled around the Canaanite soldiers, bogging their iron chariots in mud. They abandoned the chariots and ran for their lives.

It was chaos.

Barak had the advantage of speed and pursued the army all the way home. The troops of Sisera fell by the sword; not a man was left.

Then he took off after Sisera because he needed victory over this mercenary to claim the battle.

Meanwhile, Sisera arrived at Heber's house, a fugitive looking for asylum. Heber was a friend of the Canaanite king, and Sisera decided to hide out in Heber's wife, Jael's tent.

Jael came out to meet him, saying,

"Come, my lord. Come right in. Don't be afraid."

He went inside, and she hid him under a blanket.

"I'm thirsty," he said. "Please give me some water."

She opened a skin of milk, gave him a drink, and covered him up again.

"Stand in the doorway of the tent," he told her. "If anyone comes by and asks you, 'is anyone here?' say, 'No.'"

He lay down, exhausted and fell asleep.

While he lay there asleep, Jael quietly picked up a hammer and a tent peg and drove the tent peg through his temple, all the way down into the ground.

So, he died.

And Deborah's prophesy came true that God would use a woman's hand to take care of Sisera.

Unbeknown to anyone else, Jael was Deborah's second follower.

And there the dead mercenary stayed until Barak turned up. Jael walked out of her tent and up to Barak and said:

"Come and I'll show you the man you are looking for."

He followed her in to the tent and found Sisera, pinned to the ground, laid out, dead.

From that day, Deborah and her followers subdued the Canaanite king, Jabin, until there was nothing left of his rule.

Deborah's rise to be the first Jewish national leader is remembered in Jewish history as the Song of Deborah in Judges 5. It goes like this:

> When they let down their hair in Israel,
> they let it blow wild in the wind.
> The people volunteered with abandon,
> bless GOD!
>
> [3] Hear O kings! Listen O princes!
> To GOD, yes to GOD, I'll sing,
> Make music to GOD,
> to the God of Israel.

4-5 GOD, when you left Seir,
marched across the fields of Edom,
Earth quaked, yes, the skies poured rain,
oh, the clouds made rivers.
Mountains leapt before GOD, the Sinai God,
before GOD, the God of Israel.

6-8 In the time of Shamgar son of Anath,
and in the time of Jael,
Public roads were abandoned,
travellers went by backroads.
Warriors became fat and sloppy,
no fight left in them.
Then you, Deborah, rose up;
you got up, a mother in Israel.
God chose new leaders,
who then fought at the gates.
And not a shield or spear to be seen
among the forty companies of Israel.

9 Lift your hearts high, O Israel,
with abandon, volunteering yourselves with the people—bless GOD!

10-11 You who ride on prize donkeys
comfortably mounted on blankets
And you who walk down the roads,
ponder, attend!
Gather at the town well
and listen to them sing,
Chanting the tale of GOD's victories,
his victories accomplished in Israel.
Then the people of GOD
went down to the city gates.

12 Wake up, wake up, Deborah!
Wake up, wake up, sing a song!
On your feet, Barak!
Take your prisoners, son of Abinoam!

13-18 Then the remnant went down to greet the brave ones.

The people of GOD joined the mighty ones.
The captains from Ephraim came to the valley,
behind you, Benjamin, with your troops.
Captains marched down from Makir,
from Zebulun high-ranking leaders came down.
Issachar's princes rallied to Deborah,
Issachar stood fast with Barak,
backing him up on the field of battle.
But in Reuben's divisions there was much second-guessing.
Why all those campfire discussions?
Diverted and distracted,
Reuben's divisions couldn't make up their minds.
Gilead played it safe across the Jordan,
and Dan, why did he go off sailing?
Asher kept his distance on the seacoast,
safe and secure in his harbors.
But Zebulun risked life and limb, defied death,
as did Naphtali on the battle heights.

19-23 The kings came, they fought,
the kings of Canaan fought.
At Taanach they fought, at Megiddo's brook,
but they took no silver, no plunder.
The stars in the sky joined the fight,
from their courses they fought against Sisera.
The torrent Kishon swept them away,
the torrent attacked them, the torrent Kishon.
Oh, you'll stomp on the necks of the strong!
Then the hoofs of the horses pounded,
charging, stampeding stallions.
"Curse Meroz," says GOD's angel.
"Curse, double curse, its people,
Because they didn't come when GOD needed them,
didn't rally to GOD's side with valiant fighters."

24-27 Most blessed of all women is Jael,
wife of Heber the Kenite,
most blessed of homemaking women.

He asked for water,
she brought milk;
In a handsome bowl,
she offered cream.
She grabbed a tent peg in her left hand,
with her right hand she seized a hammer.
She hammered Sisera, she smashed his head,
she drove a hole through his temple.
He slumped at her feet. He fell. He sprawled.
He slumped at her feet. He fell.
Slumped. Fallen. Dead.

28-30 Sisera's mother waited at the window,
a weary, anxious watch.
"What's keeping his chariot?
What delays his chariot's rumble?"
The wisest of her ladies-in-waiting answers
with calm, reassuring words,
"Don't you think they're busy at plunder,
dividing up the loot?
A girl, maybe two girls,
for each man,
And for Sisera a bright silk shirt,
a prize, fancy silk shirt!
And a colourful scarf—make it two scarves—
to grace the neck of the plunderer."

31 Thus may all GOD's enemies perish,
while his lovers be like the unclouded sun.

The land was quiet for forty years. *

From The Message Remix Judges 5:2-31

Walking Strong

Deborah governed the nation for a peaceful forty years.

During the time she was rising in her role as national leader and over the years and decades, there were ups and downs.

Each leader stumbles and falls, experiences triumphs and disaster, sometimes in the same day.

It's important to remember that, like a hangover, neither triumphs nor disasters last forever.

They pass, and a new day arrives.

So, just try to make that new day count.

Jael, the second follower of Deborah, changed the dynamics because now Deborah with followers became a group.

The characteristics of follower-ship that Jael shows us that they are:

1. Survivors because they are adept at surviving change. They are able to adapt and conform to the situations around them, whether this means stepping up to take on an important task or quietly staying in the background.

2. Diplomatic because they have learned how to get along with those who have differences while not ignoring those differences. That's an important leadership trait, too, because a leader or manager can't afford to be oblivious to the attitudes of those around him or her.

3. Courageous because they have learned to effectively manage complication in ways that are rather similar to being a good leader. It means being engaged. It means paying attention. It means having the courage to speak up when something's wrong, and it means having the energy and activism to support a leader or manager who's doing things wisely and well.

4. Collaborators because followers are the ones who are doing much of the creative work, although the leader may get most of the credit. Leaders who have been good followers understand how to work with people to bring out the best in them.

5. Critical thinkers because they make reasoned judgments that are logical and well-thought-out. It is a way of thinking in which you don't simply accept all arguments and conclusions you are exposed to but rather have an attitude involving questioning such arguments and conclusions. Many of the same qualities that we admire in leaders, such as competence, motivation, intelligence, are the same qualities that we want in the very best followers.

A second follower makes a movement and grows very fast because when people see a group around a leader, people run to join until the small group becomes a large crowd, and a movement is established.

Like Esther and Abigail, Deborah used her strategic leadership skills to:
- Work honestly and with integrity,
- Build trust and respect,
- Lead with clarity, engagement, and accountability, and
- Enable others to learn and develop their strengths.

Questions for Reflection

Think of a leader that has inspired you and/or that has been important to you. Describe the attributes of that leader.

Ask a friend to describe your strengths.

How many attributes in your friend's description match or are similar to those you admire in others?

Do you ever wish you could see into the future?

What would be the benefits? Drawbacks?

If you had this ability, would you choose to see your own future?

History Dates

Eve	*The sixth day of creation*
Hagar	*Joined Abram's staff in* 1890s BC
Tamar	*Taken captive by Judah in* 1680s BC
Rahab	*Escaped Jericho in late* 1470s BC (R)
Naomi	*Became mother-in-law to Ruth in mid* 1270s BC
Deborah	*First Jewess national leader in* 1250s BC
Abigail	*Became the wife of David in late* 1020s BC
Bathsheba	*Became the wife of David in early* 1000s BC
Esther	*Entered a national beauty contest in* 480s BC
Elizabeth	*Became mother to John the Baptist in* 4 BC
The Samaritan Divorcee	*Became a friend of Jesus in late* 20s AD

Reference Books

Bibles

Good News Bible, Today's English Version, 1976, published by the American Bible Society and printed by The Bible Society in Australia, Canberra.

Holy Bible, New International Version (NIV), 1973, first published by the International Bible Society, Great Britain.

King James Version The Reese Chronological Bible, 1977, published by Bethany Fellowship Inc., Minneapolis, Minnesota.

New Living Translation, 2004, contained in the Cornerstone Commentary, published by Tyndale House Publishers, Illinois.

The Bible: Revised Standard Version (RSV), 1967, published by The British and Foreign Bible Society, National Churches of Christ, United States of America.

The Message/Remix, 2003, Eugene Peterson, published by Think and Navpress, Colorado Springs, Colorado.

Other Sources

ARNOLD Bill T, 2003, The NIV Application Commentary: 1 & 2 Samuel, published by Zondervan, Grand Rapids, Michigan.

ATKINSION David, 1983, The Message of Ruth: The Bible Speaks Today, published by Intervarsity Press, Nottingham, England.

BRANCH Robyn Gallaher, 2002, Deborah in the Bible published by Bible History Daily, Biblical Archeology Society.

COX V., HUDSON E., YEE G., 1994, Domestic Violence: It Doesn't Happen in our Church ... or Does It? Published by Lifecare, an activity of Baptist Community Services, Sydney, NSW.

DOUGLAS, J.D., 1962, The New Bible Dictionary Second Edition, published by Inter-Varsity Press, Leicester, England.

EDERSHEIM Alfred, 1993, The Life and Times of Jesus the Messiah, published by Henrickson's publishers, United States of America.

ELTON Ben 1999, Inconceivable, published by Black Swan, Great Britain.

FEYMER KENSEY Tikva, 1997, Hagar, The Encyclopedia of Jewish Women, updated by Tamar Kamionkowski June 23, 2021

FRYMER-KENSKY Tikva, 2004, Deborah, an extract from "Reading the Women of the Bible" published by Schocken Press.

GEARY Anna 2001 "FOUR" poem for Willow May Geary published on Facebook.

GALLARES Judette A., 1992, Images of Faith: Spirituality of Women in the Old Testament, published by MaryKnoll, Orbis Books, N.Y.

HELD EVANS Rachel G., 2018, Inspired, Slaying Giants, Walking on Water, And Loving the Bible Again, published by Thomas Nelson

HENRY Matthew, 1960, Matthew Henry's Commentary on the Whole Bible, published by Marshall Pickering, England.

JOBES Karen H, 1999, The NIV Application Commentary: Esther, published by Zondervan, Grand Rapids, Michigan.

KATHEER Ibn, 2009/1430, Stories of the Prophets from Adam to Muhammad, Dar Al-Manarah for translation, published by El-Mansoura, Egypt.

KELLS DOR Roberta, 2003, Honored, published by Fleming H Revell, Baker Book House, Grand Rapids, Michigan.

LUCADO Max, 1991, The Eye of the Storm, He Still Moves the Stones, A Gentle Thunder, published by Word Publishing, United States of America.

MINDEL Nissan, The Prophetess Deborah, published by Kehot Publication Society.

MIRREN Helen, You Tube Valediction Address

PERERA Josie, 2023, Preaching on 17 August at C3 Narara, Gosford, Australia.

PRINGLE Phil, 2012, Preaching on 5 February at C3 Oxford Falls, Sydney, Australia.

REIN Therese, 2012, Leadership, keynote speaker at Leading the Way Conference on 11 February, 2012, hosted by National Disability Services (NDS) New South Wales, funded by Family and Community Services, Ageing Disability ad Home Care, NSW Government.

SAKENFELD Katherine Doop, 2003, Just Wives? Stories of Power and Survival in the Old Testament and Today, published by Westminster John Knox Press, Louisville, London.

SIVERS Derek, 2017 How to start a Movement, TED Talk Tuesday, published by Cornerstone Rework.

SWINDOLL Charles R., 1977, A Woman of Strength and Dignity: Esther, published by World Publishing, Nashville, London, Vancouver, Melbourne.

TRITES Alison A. 2006, Cornerstone Biblical Commentary: The Gospel of Luke and Acts, published by Tyndale House Publishers, Carol Stream, Illinois.

WALTON John H, 2001, The NIV Application Commentary: Genesis, published by Zondervan, Grand Rapids, Michigan.

Bible References

Eve	Genesis 3-4; 2 Corinthians 11:3; 1 Titus 2:13
Hagar	Genesis 16-17, 21, 25; Genesis 28:29; 1 Chronicles 1:29-31; Galatians 4:21-31
Tamar	Genesis 37-38, 41-50; Ruth 4:12; 1 Chronicles 2:4
Rahab	Joshua 2-6; Psalm 114; Hebrews 11:31
Naomi	Ruth 1-4
Deborah	Judges 4 and 5
Abigail	1 Samuel 25, 27:3, 30; 2 Samuel 2:3, 3:3, 5:1-5; 1 Chronicles 3:1
Bathsheba	2 Samuel 11-12; 1 Kings 1-2; Psalm 51; Proverbs
Esther	Esther 2-9
Elizabeth	Luke 1
Divorcee	John 4

Made in the USA
Columbia, SC
02 June 2024